The Art of Living Life

Life is a work of Art.
All we need is to find the skills hidden in our very being.
The canvas of our existence was given to us at birth.
We were nurtured by others during our apprenticeship until
finally we had to take responsibility for our own masterpiece.

by
Jim Leonard

Warren Publishing, Inc.

Published by Warren Publishing, Inc.
13420 Reese Blvd. West
Huntersville, NC 28078
www.warrenpublishing.net

ISBN: 978-0-9884170-1-4

Library of Congress Control Number: 2012953033

Author at 6 months of age. 1935

Dedication

I dedicate this book to the memory of my Mom and Dad who give me Life.

My brother Frank who's life ended far too soon.

My brothers, sisters and their spouse: Tony and Rose, Eamonn and Lynn, Marie and Craig, Ann and Gill.

My children; Maureen, Pauline, Sean, Steven and Jimmy my Grand and Great Grand children, for they are the "stars" and hope of the future.

Acknowledgement

This project would not have been possible without the encouragement and support of family and friends. My deepest gratitude to Peggy, my closest friend, companion, and confidant. Her support and confidence was always present during the good times and especially those moments when it seemed just impossible to write another word. To Anna Ferro who reviewed the first draft and gave priceless structure to the outline. Marlene Monts who reviewed and edited my "final draft" and encouraged me to move forward and publish. To Ms Louise Kerz Hirschfeld, Dr Larry Kirkland and John and K.C. Picket for their generous contribution. To my many friends (too many to name) who supported this effort in many different ways.

Last but not least my wonderful editor Ms. Jere Armen and Warren Publishing President, Cathy Brophy their patience and kindness navigated me through a complex process.

Table of Contents

In the Beginning

On the day I was born I cried and my world rejoiced;
I hope I live my life that, on the day I die, the world cries and I rejoice.

—Native American proverb

THERE IS NO DOUBT that living life is a very complex and often exhausting experience. Scholars from all disciplines of the human experience have offered countless thoughts and ideas about life. Yet life can only be lived by each individual. While each culture has its own unique core beliefs, it is the individual who challenges the status quo with ideas and concepts, beliefs that were often declared heretical at the time yet from which future generations benefit greatly.

Countless numbers of human beings have been brought into this life full of the hope, dreams and expectations of their parents. Some were destined to be "stars" in the universe of human accomplishment, but most of us are only a "star" to those who love us and care for us. In the end, all "stars" fade into the vastness of the universal experience.

As the arc of my existence travels to its ultimate conclusion, I offer my life experience with the hope that it will encourage others to believe that life is worth living. Life is not a grind, although my attitude at times was just that, and on a few occasions it became so depressing that the idea of ending my life was a thought. With the help of very dear friends and family, I came to the realization that my life is no different from millions of others — yet it is uniquely mine. So my simple purpose is to tell my "story" and in doing so hopefully to allow others to understand and find their *purpose* and *passion* in life.

All living things are born into a particular moment in time.

My moment in time occurred on August 31, 1934, the oldest son of Tommy and Mary Leonard. My birth took place on a small farm outside the village of Belcoo, County Fermanagh, Northern Ireland. Our home was a typical rural Irish home of that period: built of stone with a thatched roof, a small living/dining room and two bedrooms the size of an average walk-in closet. There was no electricity or running water, and all cooking was done over an open fire in the living room. The house was placed on thirty acres of land which was so poor that it could only support one cow (which was our milk supply), a few chickens and a pig. The ground was full of rock and stone and therefore barren. Father worked as a laborer at a stone quarry, and unfortunately most of this work was done during the planting and harvesting season. Although we had a small garden in which Dad grew vegetables and a few fruits trees, the farm could not support a family of four.

During the mid-1930s the world was in the midst of the "Great Depression." Ireland had not recovered from the devastation of the Great Famine of the 19th century, and religious hatred and intolerance were rampant in Northern Ireland. In the south of Ireland, the Easter Rising of 1916 was crushed by the British Army, which at the time was in the midst of the "Great War" in Europe. That war ended in 1918, and the British Government entered into negotiations with the members of Sinn Féin, the political arm of the Irish Republican Movement. By 1921, Eire (Ireland) was granted independence from England with one major exception: Partition. As Ireland became divided and partitioned, the term "Partition" became a reality for the country.

Ireland is made up of 32 counties; citizens of the six northern counties were predominantly Protestants. The Protestants were extremely loyal to the British Crown and the families and descendants of William of Orange, of the House of Hanover. In the early 1700s, William had been invited to assume the throne of

Great Britain and Ireland to prevent a Catholic from becoming king. Catholics and Protestants at the time were engaged in bitter disputes for power and authority. So England insisted that the population of the six counties that were predominately Protestant would remain as part of the British Empire.

Ironically, in 1938, the only place that Dad could find work was in Scotland. So he left for Paisley, Scotland, and found work in Coats Industry, a spool and thread manufacturing company. Mother, my brother and I followed later, crossing the Irish Sea by ferry boat in 1939. The Second World War had already begun, and, with the British Army's retreat at Dunkirk, travel was so severely restricted that my family had to stay in Scotland for the duration of the war.

When I was five years old an incident occurred that was to influence my life immensely. It was a Sunday morning and my family and I were at Mass, where I sang in the choir. The chapel was located in a very rural part of the countryside, and people would travel from near and far by foot to meet their Sunday obligations. In those days the congregation was segregated, with women on the left and men on the right, both groups facing the church altar. I was upstairs with others in the choir. When I was in the choir loft and not singing, I was usually preoccupied with other childish behaviors, such as spending time looking down on the people below, observing the various shapes and sizes of their heads.

The women all wore various head dress. The men, on the other hand, were required to remove theirs before entering the church. (I never understood why women had to cover their heads but men uncovered theirs.) I scoured the heads of men below, looking to find one particular person: James G. Did he always blacken the top his head with shoe polish? I became aware of this after overhearing my uncles and aunts joke about him. He was bald, and I was always curious and mystified why he would do such a thing. Mass to me was mostly fun, along with singing and being upstairs and looking down on people below. On one particular Sunday morning toward the end of the Mass, the priest was interrupted by being handed a note. (Anything out of the routine of the Mass was observed by all.) The priest, with his back to the parishioners, paused for a long, long time and then slowly turned to face the congregation. In a very solemn voice he spoke:

"My dear friends, I have just been informed that Germany has bombed Poland, and many have been killed. War has come to Europe. Let us pray for the souls of the departed and recite the Rosary that this war will be over before Christmas." There was a muffled gasp throughout the chapel.

The Mass was followed by the priest leading the parishioners in reciting the Rosary. In the Irish Catholic culture for over a thousand years, the family ritual of saying the Rosary was the centerpiece of their faith. It was a faith so strong, and it was the only source of strength that allowed the Irish to survive through times of great poverty, famine and persecution.

At the conclusion of the Rosary, the priest turned and blessed the congregation, telling them to go in peace. Outside the chapel, the women and children gathered around the entrance, while the men gathered across the courtyard. There was much soft and quiet conversation taking place, and I believed this to be out of respect for the dead, for their graves were all around us. It became clear to me as I stood with my mother, listening to all this talk, that many people were afraid. Afraid of what, I wondered? My thoughts turned to God.

At various times during Mass, the priest talked to the congregation about the greatness of God. How God's son died for all our sins, and how at our baptisms we were forgiven the sin of Adam and Eve — the original sin — and that God loved us all here in this life and in the next life. So why did God let this happen, I wondered? I asked the one who knew all things, my mother. I pulled on my mother's dress to get her attention, and when she acknowledged my efforts, I asked, "Mom, why did God let this happen?" "Shush, James," she replied, followed by, "I don't know." I was stunned. S*he does not know!* If my mother does not know, then no one knows. My mother was "God" to me, so in my mind, God had nothing to do with what happened. I did not dwell on the matter too long. My thoughts returned to my surroundings as Mother was moving away from the chapel wall towards the spot where the men had gathered. My father was not there that Sunday morning as he had already left for Scotland in search of work. This, to be sure, was a very troubling time for this five-year-old boy. I was in the midst of a very Catholic region, poverty all around, father gone, with people being killed by other people. All this was happening under the protection of GOD?

Looking back on this period of my life, I now understand how I had created a "world" that was safe. Living on my grandparents' farm, I was curious about everything, and it was there that I learned how life began. I watched in amazement: a horse giving birth to a foal; a cow delivering a calf; a family of piglets scampering around their mother, fighting for a nipple to suckle; the wonder I felt while watching a hen cover her eggs or a goose protecting her nest; the excitement of watching the eggs hatch and little chicks run wildly after their mother as she pecked for food in the yard; the goslings following in single file after their mother to the pond. I not only felt the life in the animals but also in the garden as I watched vegetables sprout from the warm earth. These and many other experiences of wonder were a joy for me. I learned how life began at the farm. It would be years later before I learned how life was to be lived.

Hidden in the recesses of my mind was a struggle, a struggle that would continue for years. My mother was a saint. After my father died in 1973, Mother lived in the village not far from where she was born until she was 98. She was a devout Catholic, but more importantly she had a steadfast faith in God. Her life had been filled with both great joy and great sadness. At various times, she endured much physical pain and emotional stress. Yet throughout the long tenure of her life, she showed great love, patience and tolerance toward others. Her strength of character was so secure, and she never failed to confront any injustice she witnessed. I longed for such a faith and strength of character, never realizing that the journey of my life was all about faith, which is a necessary requirement for the development of character.

Faith is manifested in many different forms. I wanted the faith of my mother, the faith of the church, the faith of the saints, the faith of great men and women such as Mahatma Gandhi, Mother Teresa, Joan of Arc, and Mattie Stepanek, just to name a few. The dictionary defines faith as "that which is believed without any proof." As the years have gone by, I have eventually arrived at a more personal conclusion about faith: Faith is a deep personal belief that can only be understood by each individual as each experiences the consequences of his or her behavior. My behavior never lies; I just lied about my behavior. At any given point in time, my behavior, at that moment, is the truth about me. The truth, at many times, is very uncomfortable and frightening; so I lie. And when I lie, something inside me begins to die, and for me that "something" is my strength of character.

In my particular circumstances, believing was not enough. My personality and lack of character required intense work — not the kind of "work" I needed to educate myself, enhance my professional skills or interact with fellow human beings. No, it was intensive work on self-awareness, self-esteem and learning to be responsible for my own happiness, while at the same time being available to help others.

This was no easy task, and my greatest distraction was becoming discouraged. Discouragement is the enemy of success, and to the best of my knowledge we are all confronted with some form of it during our lifetimes. Even my faith did not escape the power of discouragement.

One night I felt myself being roused out of my sleep by my younger brother. “Come on, James, get up. We must go.” I was not sure if I was dreaming or had actually heard him call me. I sat up in my bed and looked around; no one was there and all was quiet, so I lay down and went back to sleep. Soon I was being shaken out of my sleep again; this time it was my mother who spoke softly to me. “James,” she said, “we must hurry and get to the air raid shelter.” I jumped out of bed, dressed hurriedly and quickly headed down three flights of stairs. Our assigned bomb shelter was located under the railroad station. As we hurried there, I listened for the sounds of airplanes flying overhead. On a couple of occasions when I did hear them, my mother assured me that that they were “ours.” I never questioned how she knew such things. We were directed to a flight of stairs that led down to what became known as a “bunker.” To me it looked more like a tunnel with a few light bulbs that provided shadowy light. I was entering into the bowels of the earth, a fascinating, mysterious and wonderful place to explore. Darkness beckoned to any Adventurer willing to face the unknown at each end of the lighted room. Only the mind of a child could make it into something safe. The other people there with us were mostly women and children and a few elderly men. We all huddled together and covered ourselves with blankets and clothing. Of course there was no heat, but we stayed warm huddled close to each other. It was my first and only “slumber” party. Years later I learned that we were on the periphery of the Blitz of 1941, Hitler’s nightly bombing raids to drive the British Isles into submission. Once settled into the shelter, I would soon be asleep again. Then when the "all clear" was given, I would be awakened and we would walk back to our homes. This nightly excursion became routine for a significant period of time, and I do not recall ever feeling afraid. Looking back to that period of my life, I now realize that faith was the absence of fear. I had complete faith (trust) in my mother.

By the time I was a young adult the only "faith" I knew was a religious faith, and it overshadowed the love of my mother. My mother always judged my behavior and chastised me when she deemed it appropriate; but she never condemned me for it. The rules of my religious indoctrination were different. Condemnation was automatic when grievous violations were committed against the church, and shame was the ultimate assassin of the individual. Over the long period of my reconstruction, I began to understand the fallacies of "Blind Faith." Blind faith, it turned out, is very different from real faith. I became aware that my "faith" was blind. There was a time when I was very vulnerable to the dictates of others. In those times of desperation I was willing to try anything to relieve the terrible agony of self-loathing. Those experiences enlightened me to the power of blind faith that man can wield over the most vulnerable.

Spiritual faith, on the other hand, is the ultimate freedom each person can achieve. Most people come to understand what is commonly known as "a spiritual awakening." There are countless ways to describe a spiritual awakening, but they all have one thing in common: *Each individual takes responsibility for what he or she believes, not what others have conditioned him or her to believe.* The idea that I, and only I, was responsible for what I believed had never entered my mind. My life was governed by the rules of the church, the culture of my ancestors, the rules of society, and family superstitions. I lived in a world where people believed they were the ultimate authority in all things. Inherent in that belief is the constant struggle among humans, the struggle for power. The history of our very existence has always been fraught with one universal question: Who is in charge? While many of us will never achieve a position of power, be it in institutions, religious entities or professional endeavors, we all have the ability to exercise power over our own lives.

In simple terms, power means *the ability to act*. It also means *to control,* but what was the source of that power? I took it for granted that the ability to control was a part of me and for me to use as I saw fit. I found myself wanting and in some circumstances needing to control others. In truth, the only person I could control was me. I did not learn that till much later in life. All human beings are born with a source of energy that gives them the power to sustain life. I was born with this power that most of us have. I had limited knowledge and skills in how to use this power. This lack of knowledge is called "ignorance," which creates fear; and fear will always misuse power to protect the self. History is full of examples of man's hunger for power, and some people believe that it is the root of evil. Ample proof exists that all religions have used power to control their followers or destroy their enemies. Despite all these horrors and misuses of power, the human species has survived and prospered. The power that sustains people is the human "spirit," best manifested in longing to be free.

I have concluded that perfect happiness is the freedom to feel truly human and truly alive, and in so doing to realize and to understand we are spiritual beings.

My Father

When I was fifteen years old, I was working two jobs, one of them with my father. Dad was the manager of a pub (bar), and on weekends I was the "bar back." This person keeps the glasses washed and beer stocked. In those days on Friday and Saturday evenings, the pubs opened at 5 p.m. and closed at 10 p.m. By 6 p.m. the bar would be full of male customers. (No women were allowed in the bar area. There was a "private room" where ladies were allowed.) By about 8 p.m. a drinking frenzy had set in, or that's what my memory recalls. Some of the patrons seemed to be aware of the time as it approached "last call," and the rate of alcohol consumption rapidly increased almost to a state of panic.

When closing time finally arrived and the last patrons had departed, some semblance of order had returned and Dad would offer the employees a drink. While the employees drank their "night cap," their conversation usually was about the night's activities and the behavior of some of the patrons. When the employees finished their drinks, they would take their leave and hurry home to their families.

My dad and I were alone. As he finished the task of counting the night's receipts and securing the premises, he and I would talk. I would usually ask questions about the evening's events. Dad would explain why such-and-such an action might have taken place that evening. I remember little of our conversations, but I will always treasure those times when I was in his company and it was just Dad and me.

British money in those days came in all shapes and sizes and from different banking establishments. Bank of Scotland, Bank of England, and Commercials Bank each produced their own paper money, using different colors and designs to identify their particular bank notes. Bank of England notes were accepted anywhere. Other banks' notes were either not accepted in some transactions or, if they were, there was an added fee. However, in Dad's pub that rule did not apply; money was good regardless of which bank issued it. So I watched my father count the coins and sort out the paper money by its color, denomination, and relevant bank.

I remember the first time I really paid attention to this process. As Dad stacked the money, I noticed a slight grin on his face. What was Dad smiling about? He told me that the owner of the pub was extremely superstitious about the color green. His wife was not allowed to have anything in the house that was green. He would not eat any green vegetables nor would he wear any clothing that had the slightest hint of green. He even avoided walking on green grass, and therefore there was no grass around his house.

As Dad completed stacking the paper money, he would always put the green-colored notes on top. The owner really loved my dad and had the utmost confidence in my father's integrity and honesty. On many an evening, my dad would bring home the night's receipts. The owner would send a message saying when he was going to stop by and pick up the money. On this particular evening when the owner stopped by the pub, my father introduced me to him, and after the customary pleasantries my dad placed the money on the counter of the bar, with the green paper placed on top of all the others. The owner's reaction was hilarious when I think of it now, but that night it startled me. The owner, with a stick or wooden ruler, knocked the green money off the top of the stack, picked up all the other bills with his hand and placed them in his brief case. With the wooden ruler he scooped the green money into a paper bag. He was not happy with my dad, and he scowled about something and left. Dad just smiled and we headed home. I was flabbergasted at what I had seen. Dad told me not to worry, that it was a little game they played with each other many times. My father at one time offered the owner a solution. “John,” he said, “tell you what. You don't have to pay me each week. I will take all the green notes off your hands each week and that will solve your problem. As for me, it will be a great motivation to do more business for you.” John never responded, and Dad never spoke of it again.

As the years have gone by, the memories of my father bring tremendous comfort to my heart and peace to my mind. I treasured those nights after work as he and I would walk home after we closed the pub. I had no way of knowing that, a couple of years later, I would be crossing the Atlantic, never to experience those moments again.

I remember on a couple of occasions on our way home Dad and I would pass a building and there in the entrance would be a man sleeping. I would ask Dad why the man was doing that. He would reply, “God bless them, son. The drink has got them.” The impact on me, the first time I heard those words, was inescapable. When I would go to work with my dad, I was usually excited as I watched men being men. Drinking, talking and enjoying the moment. Now I began to see the dark side of alcohol, and I was sure at an unconscious level it would never happen to me. I felt sadness as I recognized that once in a while the individual sleeping in the entrance was someone I had served a drink to at one time or another. These men began to present themselves as something other than “men.” Were they weaklings, useless and a disgrace to their families, or was I contributing somehow to their downfall?

Years later I was to find myself in exactly in the same position as those men. Today I am aware it was not who served me the drink that contributed to my “downfall.” The choice to drink was mine and mine alone, and, once I took a couple of drinks of alcohol, I lost the ability to stop drinking of my own "free" will. The thought that I had lost the power of choice in drinking was impossible for me to consider, but someone or something was responsible for my downfall. And so began the long, arduous journey to find the cause of my unhappiness.

My father was a gentle, kind, pragmatic man and the wisest person I ever knew. I could not see how my father's profession and his way of earning a living contributed to the condition of these men. He was always ready to help the less fortunate, even in those days when most of us lived under very harsh conditions, with food and fuel shortages and money so short that paying for electrical power was done on an "as needed" basis. Many other basic amenities which are now considered routine, such as personal telephones and central heating, were not available.

Earlier in my life I experienced a conflict with God; now another conflict was added to my inner turmoil. Although mentally I refused to accept that my father's work had anything to do with what was happening to these men, deep down there was a nagging question: Why was I feeling that these men and their drunkenness was my fault?

After I turned fifteen years old, with the help of my father I found a position with a company that built and installed fireplaces in peoples' homes. My employer was a very devout, religious man. He belonged to a church called Jehovah's Witness. I had no idea what that was, and none of my friends knew either. He was a gentleman and never swore. The only thing I heard him say in frustration was "Oh, my Gordon Highlander!" I knew he was upset, but "Gordon Highlander"? They were a famous Scottish regiment. I could not see the correlation. Later I realized that it was his way of expressing anger or frustration. Very quickly I learned my trade, and by the age of sixteen I was promoted to team leader. I usually had one or two men assisting me as we installed a fireplace. Each week I would receive my pay in a small, brown envelope containing the sum of money I had earned that week. I would give my pay envelope to my mother, and she in turn would give me 5 shillings, the equivalent to $1.00 at the time.

To this day I have no idea how much I was paid each week. I worked six days a week and never saw the contents of my pay envelope. It never occurred to me to ask my mother how much money was in the envelope; she was my mom and her love for me was absolute. It would be some years later before I realized what my parents had done with some of my hard-earned pay.

On Sunday mornings during spring, summer and fall, my dad and I would set out to our family "victory" garden. It was a project initiated early in the war effort so that we could become more self-sustaining by growing our own vegetables for our family and for other families who were unable to grow their own vegetables in their own gardens. These garden plots, as they were called, were provided by the town, and each participant was responsible for its use and maintenance. We grew a variety of fruits and vegetables, such as lettuce, cabbage, tomatoes, potatoes, beans, peas, carrots, blackberries, strawberries, and rhubarb. It was here that I learned the basic facts of life — but never fully understood them until much later in my life. Father, in the simple wisdom of a farmer, taught me the purpose of "amending" the soil. "James," he said, "you must take care of the soil, and it will provide you the food for your body. The soil gives up a lot of energy so that our garden will produce a good crop of vegetables and fruit. We, on the other hand, must cooperate with the soil by replacing the used energy. We do this by adding nutrients, by applying mulch, and every so often we let a section of our garden rest." He explained "That's why nothing is to be discarded or deemed useless in this garden. This can be hard work for us, but remember, the earth works hard also. That is the cycle of life."

The walk to our garden and back home was about five miles

or more. First we went to Mass, then to our garden. It would be early afternoon before we returned home. Mother always had Sunday dinner ready for us at that time. It was a masterful feat and a wonderful feast since food was very scarce. My brothers, sisters and I would sit at the dinner table with great anticipation and excitement. What work of magic would Mom perform today? Our excitement was further enhanced by the wonderful aromas drifting from her small kitchen stove. A vision of that small room drifts back with memories from long ago.

We lived in a third-floor flat, and the front door opened into a small hallway which led to four doors. The first door on the right opened into a room that contained the living room, kitchen and bedroom. On the wall immediately to the right was space for a small stove, and beyond that were a window and the kitchen sink. The back wall had a small coal fireplace and on each side was space for a radio and some of Mom's knick-knacks. The third wall contained an alcove, in which our parents' bed was located. During the day, the bed was hidden by a handmade curtain, and to the left of that curtain, against the wall, was a fold-down leaf table that was primarily used for Sunday dinners or for when guests arrived. In order to ensure we had sufficient electricity for the house lights and other small electrical appliances, there was a black box in the hallway. In that box we would insert coins to pay for our electrical supply. Money, being a rare commodity, forced all of us into an austere life style. Radio use was limited to news about the war; sometimes we used candles to provide light. Our family activities took place in this environment, and in this tiny home there existed a happiness that I was to spend thirty years trying to recapture. And recapture I did.

One particular Sunday afternoon when I was seventeen, my family settled down for one of Mother's great moments of magic. My father sat at the head of the table; I was at the opposite end. On either side sat my brothers and sisters. Mother's place was immediately to the left of my dad and closest to the stove. The meal was scrumptious: pure white, whipped garden-grown potatoes blended with fresh milk and creamery butter; beautiful sliced roast beef with dark brown gravy; and an assortment of red beets, green peas, and fresh carrots. There was also fresh-baked bread and plenty of soft butter. In small glasses she poured the water in which she had cooked the peas and carrots. Dad loved to drink that vegetable juice. We did the same — albeit, for some of us, reluctantly.

Everything Mother served was steaming hot and out of this world. We always waited until Mom had everything on the table, then we would bow our heads and Dad would recite the following prayer, "Bless us, O Lord, and these thy gifts which we are about to receive from your bounty, through Christ our Lord. Amen." Once in a while he would say, "Eat up and give this house a good name." (It would be years later before I understood its significance.) When the main course of this meal was finished (our plates were always clean of food) and we were about to receive dessert, my dad looked straight at me and said, "James, how would you like to go to America?" I was stunned. There was a long pause, and all my brothers and sisters stopped talking and were now staring at me. My mother was standing beside dad with a plate in her hand and a beautiful smile on her face. I could not think. I looked at my father's face and there was a whimsical look, like, *Well, I am waiting*. The air rushed out of my lungs, carrying forward the word "Yes." Dad looked up at my mother and said, "Well, Mary, that's settled. What's for dessert?"

Somewhere between three and six months later, everything was prepared for my trip to America. The excitement and anticipation were so overwhelming that I have no recollection of going through the motions of getting a passport, visa, health records and other immigration documents necessary for admission into the United States. My father bade me farewell at the train station in Paisley, Scotland. I departed with my mother and brother for Belcoo, Ireland, the place of my birth. There I finished whatever last-minute arrangements were necessary, bade farewell to my grandparents and other family members, and set out by car from my grandparents' small home in County Fermanagh for a long drive to Cork City, in the south of Ireland. There I would board a tender boat to be taken to a ship anchored in the outer harbor.

On the long ride south to Cork City I was full of all kinds of emotions, but as we got closer to our destination, one emotion was to repress all other emotions: excitement, an excitement that was enhanced by the wonderful fantasies I created in my mind about crossing the Atlantic and reaching America's shores. Once on board I would sail far beyond the horizon to live my dream. Surely I would accomplish what millions of others had done before me: immigrate to a land of milk and honey, a land of prosperity and gold, a land of great men and women, a land of geniuses — America, a place where all men were created equal, the land of the free and home of the brave.

It was years later that I recalled the scene of the lonely figure of my mother on the quay, watching as she saw her first-born disappear over the horizon, unsure if she would ever see her son again. Only then did I fully understand the sacrifices my mother constantly made to take care of her children and now this ultimate, bittersweet sacrifice. I have often wondered what those months leading up to my departure had been like for her.

Coming to America

The journey across the Atlantic took ten days. First we stopped at Halifax, Nova Scotia, then on to New York. My berth was in the lowest deck on ship, a small cabin with seven other men. There were a couple of fellows from South Africa, two from England, a Scotsman, and a father and son who, I found out later, were from Poland. The father and son were fascinating people to me. Their language was strange. I could recognize French, German, Italian and Spanish, but the tongue they spoke was very unusual and at times made more confusing, for I became acutely aware that they spoke in more than one dialect. Their dress was also different, always black and white. The father and son wore a black hat that I was to come to know as a yarmulke. Finally I got the courage to strike up a conversation with the boy. The father quickly joined it. To my astonishment they spoke wonderful English, with a very pronounced accent.

The boy and I became close friends, and we would wander the deck of the ship, curious about its structure and the people on board. I noticed that his father was always close by, never leaving his son out of his sight, yet allowing him some freedom to be with me. One beautiful day the father, his son and I were on the deck as the ship glided gently over a very calm ocean. I don't recall how the discussion started, maybe he asked me about my family. I recall asking the father where they were from. "Poland," he replied. "Why are you going to America?" I asked. "To start a new life," he answered. There was a long pause. I remembered when the priest said that the war had started, and Poland was being bombed by Germany in September, 1939. Now it was July of 1952, thirteen years later. "Was it bad during the war?" I asked somewhat sheepishly. He looked away for a long time, and then whispered, "Yes." As he spoke, he was looking longingly at his young son. I waited, not daring to ask another question, but knew deep within there was more to come. He told me he grew up in Poland. That he was from a Jewish family that had been arrested and thrown into Auschwitz. He and his son were the only members of his family to survive. The full impact of this statement was to be driven home by his further explanation that in the village where he grew up were many members of his extended family. All of them had been lost in the Holocaust. When he had finished his story, his son rose from where he was sitting and nestled into his father's lap. For the rest of the afternoon until dinner time we sat in silence.

That evening I sat alone on the deck. A dance was taking place in the small ballroom; the sound of music, laughter and happy fellowship drifted out over the deck toward the vast moonlit ocean. I thought of a newspaper article I had read a few days after the end of the war. Pictures of the horrors of Bergen-Belsen concentration camp flew off the page. I could barely comprehend the evil I saw, bodies stacked upon each other, nothing but skin and bone. The lifeless expression on their faces spoke volumes of the horrors they had endured before the relief of death.

There on deck, with the beauty of the night as far as the eye could see, the joy of living resonated in my ears from sounds of happy people. The serenity that covered the world that night was in striking contrast to the images in my mind. The tragedy of my new friends' experiences and the memory of those pictures made me cry out again, "Why?" My perception of life and faith in fellow human beings was being slowly torn asunder. A profound sadness came over me. I did not know it at the time, but the events in my life would lead me to many moments of sadness and deep depression. It became a profound realization later in my life.

The next day life was back to reality. I had won the ship's lottery by correctly guessing the distance we had traveled in the previous 24 hours. So I shared my great fortune with my young Polish friend and a young German girl. The young girl, whose name I can never remember, was so beautiful and innocent that at first I was nervous when in her presence. But somehow I became more relaxed as each day went by.

Part of my shyness was created prior to leaving home. I had met a young Scottish girl. She was tall, beautiful in stature, and had the most gorgeous smile I had ever seen. We dated by going to the pictures (movies) and dances. Unfortunately, she lived a long way from home, and if we missed the last bus, I would walk her home, then return to my own house. Of course, this meant I would get home very late. When my parents found out that I was dating, they became very concerned. They reluctantly allowed me to do this once a week but under the strict condition that I would be home by 11:00 p.m. Of course, young love would never accept that, and as I got closer to my departure date to America, every moment being with her was invaluable to me.

During the last week before I left for America came a beautiful summer night with a full moon. I don't recall whether we went to a movie or a dance. As we walked to the bus stop, I was very aware that this would be our last night together. We found a secluded doorway where we held each other, kissed longingly and passionately, and spoke words of love. The bus came and left. As it drove off, we looked at each other, smiled, and held each other. No other act of intimacy occurred, although my body longed for her. It was never an option, and we both understood that. An hour or two went by, and that dreadful moment arrived. It was time to take her home. The walk to her home was a long and happy adventure.

As we approached her home, the light was on in her house, and I knew that her parents were waiting for her. I took her to her door but did not enter; instead, I started running so that I would not to have to confront her parents, yet also knowing I was going to be confronted by my own parents. Sure enough, both of them were up. After being questioned about where I had been, who I had been with, and what we had been up to, I was given a severe lecture by my dad about responsibility. Confused and, I suspect, somewhat hurt, I was sent to bed. What I could not figure out was that I was about to leave in a few days for America. I believed I had been a loyal and faithful son. I think I cried myself to sleep that night. Today I know exactly what my parents had felt that night. It was not that they were angry at me; on the contrary, they loved me dearly, and I was about to leave them.

Because my sense of loyalty was so deep, based on my family values, any thought other than friendship with my young German friend was out of the question. Besides, it was made easy by the fact she could not speak English and I could not speak German. We soon discovered that we could communicate in ways other than speech, and in doing so we had a wonderful time for the rest of the trip. Before long we were sailing up New York Harbor, and as the ship slid past the Statue of Liberty, a profound silence came over the ship. Even the sound of its engines seemed to disappear.

The morning sun had just begun to rise over the New York City skyline. The waters of the harbor were calm, so calm that they reflected the skyline like a glass mirror. During the previous evening Immigration Officials had boarded the small ship, interviewed the passengers, checked their papers and cleared all for entry to the United States. When the officials departed, the passengers were informed that it was too late to continue up the harbor to the docking quay. Feeling disappointed, I went to bed and tried to sleep. Anticipation and excitement, however, did not allow much sleep. Before dawn I arose from my bunk, surprised to discover that most of the other passengers had already gone up to the upper deck.

Dawn was breaking as I reached the upper deck. The ship's captain had raised anchor, and we were now gliding over a sheet of water. As the waters parted gracefully like the opening of mother's arms to accept her children, my excitement reached an unbearable crescendo. As we gently sailed past the Statue of Liberty, not a sound was to be heard, not even the cry of the sea gulls as they escorted us up the harbor. The powerful engines of our ship seemed to be silent in humble admiration. We, the passengers, were completely overwhelmed emotionally by the majesty of that incredible structure and what it meant to many of us. "*Give me your tired, your poor, your huddled masses yearning to breathe free.*"

Ten days crossing the Atlantic on board this wonderful ship was an incredible experience for this 17-year-old boy who had boarded her in Cork, Ireland. And now I was about to realize my greatest dream: America.

Aunt Annie, my father's only sister, was there to greet me. I had met her once when she came to visit my family. I never really liked her, or so I thought at the time. Years later, as I got to know and understand her, I realized that what I truly felt for her was sadness, a feeling I was to experience many times in my life. But I also discovered that all human beings experience sadness sometime in their lives. After the dutiful embrace, Aunt Annie and I left the dock and boarded a subway to New York City. (It was years later when I found out we had docked in Yonkers, a couple miles north of Manhattan.)

I was eager to see New York, but first I was to experience my first subway ride aboard the New York subway system: a noisy, clunky, swaying ride that eventually ended in Manhattan. While exiting the station to the streets of the city, I was halfway up those stairs when I suddenly stopped: coming down hurriedly was a man in a trench coat, collar turned up, carrying what looked like a violin case. I immediately knew he was a member of Al Capone's gang. After all, I had seen someone just like this person in a newsreel or movie and he was working for Mr. Capone. I backed up against the wall as he scurried past me.

Arriving at the top of the subway entrance, I stepped into the new world to a breathtaking wonder: New York City. Its huge tall skyscrapers, flags flying from buildings, yellow taxi cabs, people hurrying here and there, and cars . . . I had never seen so many cars in one place. There was excitement in the air. People were happy and seemed to be enjoying each other. The sun was warm, and its rays constantly danced off the tall buildings like flash bulbs from a thousand cameras. I saw several newspaper stands where people were selling their wares. The city, its people, its life was intoxicating; and I drank it all up. The dreariness of my past was gone.

My aunt, God bless her, tried to make me feel at home. What she never fully understood was that I *was* at home. All my life, regardless of where I am, I have always been *at home*. Of course she had no way of knowing that.

When I was young, I left school to work at learning a trade and, more importantly, to help my family. I was a dreamer. I had been a dreamer since I was five years old. Even then I had concluded that God was not going to protect the world, and I had to make a choice: create evil or create good. Life has now taught me that evil is simply the word "live" spelled backwards. The reality is that each of us must learn the basic concepts of good and evil through trial and error. Our parents can only prepare us as best they can for what life will bring us. At some point, we must each take responsibility for the choices and decisions that we make every day. To deny such responsibility is the core of all that is evil. But what is responsibility? I would argue that, in the simplest of terms, it means the ability to respond. I have come to believe my parents instilled basic understanding of its use, but in many instances I chose not to use it. The consequence of those choices was to develop a reactionary response.

In what I call my period of innocence, I believed that all people were good. Those like Hitler were somehow not human, therefore evil. I believed that America was the epitome of goodness; America had saved the world, defeated evil empires, and brought peace and hope to the world.

My Early America Experience

My aunt and I left New York City by bus bound for Newton, MA, to visit some distant relatives. A few days later we arrived in Schenectady, NY. My aunt, who worked in the parish rectory, had located a small room for my living accommodations with a Mr. and Mrs. Kelly. They were wonderful people, who provided a cozy room for me until I got settled and located work. My first full day in Schenectady was one I will never forget. I arose at dawn, got dressed, and set out to see my surroundings. Schenectady's major industry at the time was General Electric, and I recall there were also a company that built army tanks and a hotel that was under construction.

I had no idea where I was going that morning; I just wanted to see the town. At a major intersection downtown, I came across a diner, the kind that resembled a silver bus. It was a stainless-steel structure with small windows, each covered by a canopy. I had seen similar diners in movies. With the exception of one empty counter stool at the far end, the diner was filled with people. A juke box played music while everyone was talking. I decided to occupy the empty seat.

There were half a dozen or more booths in the diner, each of them occupied. Behind the counter was a young girl about my age. Behind her in the center of the back wall was an opening where the girl would convey her customers' requests to someone in the back whose responsibility it was to cook and prepare the meals. It seemed to me she was constantly moving and calling out various orders, and the man behind the back wall at times would say such things as "pick up" or a few other remarks that I felt had nothing to do with food.

I entered the diner with some trepidation and shyness and slowly walked to the empty stool, all the time avoiding eye contact with others. I sat down and waited. Before long a girl approached and asked, "What you will have?" She was a pretty girl. So pretty that I could hardly look at her, and I did not understand why. Without looking up I replied, "I would like a cup of hot tea please." "Will there be anything else?" she asked. "No," I said. With that she was off, soon to return with cup and saucer in hand, which she laid on the counter in front of me, and said, "Will there be anything else?" "No, thanks," I replied. In the blink of an eye she was gone. I looked at the cup in front of me, and to my surprise it contained only hot water. I immediately thought she had made a mistake but almost as quickly changed my mind to think, How could she? She is too pretty to do such a thing. It must have been my accent. Ah, that's it: she misunderstood. My thoughts were interrupted by her voice. "Is there something wrong?" she asked. "Yes. I asked for hot tea and you brought me hot water." "I brought you your tea," and she was off again. I sat there staring into the cup of hot water. I became aware that a man sitting on the stool to my right was watching all of this. He did not say a word, but I was convinced that he believed I was stupid.

When you're seventeen, just two days in the country of your dreams, in a conversation with a beautiful young lady, and you feel you're losing control, it is natural that you become more nervous, especially when there is an "old bull" watching. By now, the dynamics of the encounter had changed. It had become a triangle and an internal struggle. The struggle was complicated by a multitude of feelings, each one becoming stronger than the others. It appeared that time was suddenly speeding up, and in my desperation I wanted time to slow down. I needed "time" to think so I could somehow grasp each one of these feelings and deal with it, repeat the process and, when finished, make the appropriate and intelligent response. After all, isn't that what adults are supposed to do?

A voice interrupted my thoughts. "Is there something wrong?" she asked. Immediately I was aware of who and what was around me. I sat straight up in my stool. In a cool, clear voice, with clarity in words so as not to let my Scottish dialect confuse her, I said, "Yes. I had ordered a cup of tea, and you brought me water." "I brought you tea," she said. With that she reached with her fingers behind my cup, grasped a string and slowly began to lift it high above my cup. At the end of the string was a small bag. Like one of those huge construction cranes, the waitress directed the bag over the top of my cup, and then lowered it into the hot water. Dunk, dunk, dunk, and, low and behold, the water slowly changed into tea. I was stunned. I had never seen a tea bag before.

An entirely new set of feelings gathered. Again I was at the mercy of their cumulative effect. Anxiety — I did not know at the time that's what it was. In my mind it was my stupidity. I had come to believe that somehow I should have known that which I did not know. For the next twenty-five years, my life would be at the mercy of this self-imposed truth.

I stared at her, my face red with embarrassment, not knowing what to say. With her hands on her hips, a twinkle in her eye, head thrown back, and a "gotcha" smile on her face, "Will there be anything else?" she asked. Trying to recover myself, save face, exert my manhood, whatever it was, I found myself looking on the wall behind her. In those days the menu was on the wall in bright colors, greens and blues and reds. "Yes," I replied. My voice trailed off as I pondered the assortment of menu options on the wall behind her. As I looked, I began to feel those emotions return. There were things listed there I had never seen or heard of before, such as hot and cold cereal, flap jacks, waffles, and the like. There was the standard fare of bacon and eggs, etc. Alas, it was too late. I was mesmerized by these assortments of foods. My thoughts were broken by the sound of her voice. "Well, what shall it be?" Her tone was somewhat stressed. My God, I thought. Suppose I order something and, when I get it, I don't know what it is. "Well?" she said again. I took a deep breath, sat straight up and looked at her square in the eye. "I know what I want," and with a clear, strong voice I said "I think I would like a piece."

Almost instantaneously there was a stunned silence in the restaurant. The girl's face blushed red, the man sitting beside me stopped eating, his fork suspended in mid-air, with yellow yolk from his egg dripping onto his plate. Then pandemonium broke out. I heard voices shouting "Throw the so-and-so out." The man, with egg dripping from his fork, reached out and grabbed me around the neck with his left hand, yanked me off the stool and slung me into the booth behind me. The next thing I knew was that I was being hustled to the door, and there two others grabbed me and literally threw me out onto the street.

Lying in the middle of the street in my Sunday-best clothes, fighting back tears, the one person I wanted was three thousand miles away — my mother. As people on their way to work walked around this pitiful sight, I was to experience another overwhelming feeling, one that I was to revisit many times over the next thirty years of my life. I experienced isolation so devastating that, with each experience, the ability to think became increasingly difficult. The feeling of fear intensified until that feeling was replaced by deep isolation and loneliness. I subsequently became aware that many others who had reached such depths of despair thought of death as the ultimate relief.

During the war, when I would return home from school, I would call out to my mother, saying, "Hi, Ma, I'm home; throw me a piece." She would respond by throwing out the window a sandwich wrapped in newspaper. The sandwich was made of two slices of black bread covered with a light spreading of lard sprinkled with sugar. It was a "piece sandwich" and, just like kids all over, I dropped the word "sandwich" and asked for a "piece." That morning in the diner I knew exactly what I was asking for. Some years later I found out what the word "piece" meant in America — and it was a heck of a lot better than that darn sandwich I had been eating.

My first job was in the local A&P supermarket. How that occurred was one of those many "coincidences" that happened throughout my life. I had entered the store to inquire about work.

The person who spoke to me explained that hiring was done at their Human Resources Office in Albany, New York. However, she pointed to the store manager, who was having a conversation with a gentleman at the dairy products case. I decided to go over and ask him if there was anything he could do. He was very kind and, after listening to me, apologized for not being able to help me. However, he invited me to come back later and see what could be done. As I turned to walk away, the man with whom the manager had been conversing called out to me. "Young man, what is your name?" "James Leonard," I replied. "Where are you from?" he asked. "Ireland, sir," says I. "What part?" says he. "Co. Fermanagh, sir," says I. "Where in Co. Fermanagh?" says he. My curiosity was beginning to rise. "The village of Belcoo," I replied. "Young man, my name is also Leonard, and my father was from that part of the country." At this point, he turned to the store manager and said something to the effect that something could be found for me at the store. It was a coincidence that Mr. Leonard was the regional manager for A&P in upstate New York. The next day I took a bus to Albany, where I completed application forms, and started work the following Monday. Working there was a lot of fun for me. I was exposed to every department: dairy, meat, produce and store room. The only position I did not fill was that of cashier at the checkout stand.

I looked forward everyday to going to work and my enthusiasm combined with my work ethic boded well for me. It was not too long before I was the "star" employee. Across the street from the store was a grill that served meals, and in the first few weeks on the job, I think I ate there every day. I tried various dishes and always had dessert afterwards. After a month or so of eating at the grill, one morning I bent down to pick up a can that had fallen off the shelf. That was the last thing I remember. I awoke in the emergency room, but, after a complete check up, I was sent home. The next day I was told to rest a few days and cut back on my menu. Apparently my stomach was so small that I had over-taxed it with large meals that overwhelmed my body's capacity to process in a normal manner. The doctor said it was the most unusual case he had ever seen. He informed me that his best guess was that my stomach had adjusted to the limited food supply that had been available during and after the war.

I worked there for almost two years. It was a wonderful experience that I will never forget. Alas, a recession set in, and my hours were reduced to part-time. I arranged my schedule to allow myself to go to high school, but I could not adjust to the high school culture. I was nineteen years old, and I felt very odd and clumsy amongst the senior class. It was most embarrassing as I was trying to make up for the four years of high school I had missed. It became overwhelming, so I dropped out.

After one year, as I was settling in to my new career at the A&P Supermarket, an incident occurred that propelled me into another phase of my life. At a company outing everybody was having a wonderful time. I had become the center of attraction at my first experience of a "clambake." Scooping clams from their shells and letting them slide down your throat was not something that impressed me. Many of the guests wanted to hear about my homeland, the war, growing up in Scotland, and my strange accent. Of course their excitement grew as they explained some of their food items, specifically ones that I had never seen. Corn on the cob was new to me, and I enjoyed it as I did many other sundry food items displayed on a long table. Ah, but the dessert counter! Pies of all descriptions, cakes of various shapes, ice cream in many flavors, and other delicious items my eyes had never seen before. I was having the time of my life, and people had embraced me and welcomed me into their midst.

During the course of the day, people began to assemble at the bar. Others had taken their children home. Still others had taken their leave from the festivities and departed for other places. In the end, a small group had congregated at the bar, and there was lots of merriment and laughter. This wonderful demonstration of conviviality and friendship was new, strange and exciting to me.

My ride home was there, and I was completely relaxed in this wonderful atmosphere.

I ended up in the company of a few of my fellow workers, who, it must be pointed out, were female. There was a lot of laughter and giggling going on, and the conversation had become more personal. By this time I was trapped between two women, and I sensed that the topic of the conversation was me. I remember one of the girls was about my age, tall and very statuesque. The other lady was much older than I was, slim, with long black hair and deep dark eyes that sparkled with tiny bolts of lightning. I had been drinking orange juice. However, both had suggested that I put something in it and join the party. I resisted. By now both of these ladies had brushed up against me with their bodies. I assumed this had happened because of the congestion of people at the bar. Soon I was squeezed tight between them. Strange sensations began to overwhelm me. I could feel myself panicking, feeling out of control.

I wanted to run, but at the same time I wanted to cling to them like a powerful magnet. My throat was dry; I could not speak; my face was flushed. I reached for the orange juice one of the women had handed me and took a large gulp. It tasted different. I looked at the glass strangely but was told it was a different kind of orange juice. With that, I drank it all.

What occurred after drinking the orange juice is very blurred in my memory. I am confused as to what was fact or fantasy. Suffice it to say both women by now became very intimate with me in very subtle ways. They were caressing my ears and neck, running their hands up and down my legs. They took my hands and placed them in various parts of their body including some very personal areas. I was ecstatic with pleasure, a pleasure I had never known. I knew that my heart would burst and my body explode, yet strangely was not afraid. I was "rescued" from this wonderful experience by the store manager, who apparently had some idea what was going on and decided to step in.

On the way home, I apparently acted silly in conversation.

What I was to find out later was I was drunk. I drank no alcohol after that for a long time. However, when I joined the local amateur soccer club, the coach suggested I drink a bottle of German beer daily in an effort to put on weight. There was no other logical reason to drink more than that at the time. Later, however, I seemed to have lost all logical thinking regarding the amount I would drink after a couple of drinks.

Intimacy is a necessary part of life. Without it, life as I know it would be different. While I believe that most people have a general idea of what intimacy is, they are often afraid or unsure of it. My experiences with my dad, the event at the diner, and now the clambake experience were profound moments of intimacy at different levels. In each instance, the essential elements of human life were affected: physical, mental and emotional. For most of the first fifty years of my life, there were numerous times when I was uncomfortable and uneasy interacting with others. Any time the conversation implied or specified intimacy, I felt trapped and wanted to escape. I finally discovered I had a distorted idea of the meaning of intimacy. Any thought or inquiry about sex was taboo in the environment where I grew up. This attitude may appear simplistic for many. I believe that intimacy blooms completely when, in a relationship, one has a sense of belonging and participation and is recognized by those companions and fellow human beings involved in the relationship. And that may be "reaching" the ultimate in human intimacy. I have come to believe that others desire the same kind of intimacy.

My Professional Career

I was aware that I had not met my military obligations to the United States and therefore it would be a number of years before I could apply for US Citizenship. The answer to meeting these military obligations was to enlist in the United States Air Force, which I did, and fifteen months later, in Frankfurt, Germany, I was sworn in as a citizen of the United States. My military commitment took longer to complete.

After I enlisted in the US Air Force, I was stationed at Samson Air Base in upstate New York for Basic Training. The most difficult experience during that period was the constant harassment I received from a group of men from Alabama. My assigned training unit included a fellow from Bangor, ME, about seventy men from various parts of Alabama, and me. They could not understand my mixture of Irish and Scottish accent. So they set about trying to "motivate" me to learning their form of English, which at times I could not understand. Their methods of motivation included that I memorize and recite my General Orders (and when I did recite them, of course, they could not understand me). My training consisted of assigned detail duty of scrubbing the wooden steps at the entrance to the barracks and the floor in the hallway using toothbrushes (which I had to pay for). I also received a lot of extra fire-watch drill from 2:00 a.m. till 4:00 a.m., which of course disrupted my sleep pattern. Other "exercises" included marching with my M1 Carbine held over my head, walking the block for thirty minutes, and other sundry details. As I reflect on those experiences, I know I learned the foundation of tolerance through determination — a virtue that would become indispensable in later years.

I spent eighteen weeks at Samson AFB and at Westover AFB

in Massachusetts, where I assisted in the transfer of my unit to McGuire AFB in New Jersey. I had just settled into military duty when I was reassigned to Sembach Air Base, in Germany. There I received my greatest achievement: I was sworn in as citizen of the United States and reassigned to Prestwick Air Station, in Scotland, which was only 28 miles from my parents' home in Paisley, Scotland. My first four years of active duty were incredible.

The only girl I ever dated before my immigration to the US was to become the mother of my three sons and two daughters. She was a wonderful woman, beautiful, strong in character and faith. I will always be grateful to her for her strength and perseverance during a very tumultuous period of my life. In spite of her sufferings in our relationship, five wonderful children have grown up to be successful human beings in all aspects of their lives. Despite their own hardships and struggles, my children have endured life with dignity and integrity, so much so that I am the proud grandfather of sixteen grandchildren and six great-grandchildren. However, during their youth I was not mentally or emotionally capable of providing sound parental guidance. My children's mother was their model of strength and teacher of character, and for that I shall always remain grateful.

I had turned twenty years old. I was now a man. Before leaving home, my father had only a few requests that I should fulfill. One of those requests was that I refrain from drinking alcohol until I was twenty-one. I remember kneeling before my dad as he blessed me by placing his hand on my head. I was somewhat startled by this demonstration of intimacy and became oblivious to everything around me. It was an experience that laid the foundation for my spiritual life, and at that time I had no concept of a spiritual life. There would be many future moments when I felt I had disappointed my father by failing to live up to his blessings and become the man he thought I could be.

When I look back at my relationship with my parents, I am convinced it was the foundation for how I would interact with others in various relationships. As I child, my father and mother were my "God." They were everything to me: my protectors, my instructors, my directors, my healers. I did not have to confess to them, for they knew things about my character that even I did not know. They even anticipated thoughts and actions that I would take before I did them. They were incredible. They were so wonderful that I could not imagine how my mother and father (in their moment of sweet intimacy) created me. They were so powerful they just wished me and there I was.

I retired from active duty after completing twenty-three years of active service in September, 1977. A year later I was hired by a company to develop and implement an alcoholism treatment program at a local hospital. Although I had no knowledge of hospital administration, I had some experience in mid-level management, which I had acquired while on active duty. I was also a recovering alcoholic, with over two years of abstinence from alcohol use.

Thus began a new career in which I had no formal education but a strong motivation to help others. To balance my commitment to the patient and my obligation to the company was very stressful. In many instances I was unsure if I would survive the stress. During my military career, when faced with such stress, a drink would bring relief. I could no longer afford that luxury; I had to replace dependence on a liquid, alcohol, with the reliance on the wisdom of others. And it worked. However, to understand "wisdom" requires a major shift in one's thinking process. Although I had developed a reputation as a dedicated employee, after two years I was asked to resign from the company.

The request to resign was a terrible shock. Business was good, the staff was exceptional, and the bottom line was always above budget. To be fired at forty-five years old and three years into a civilian career was devastating. The test of my emotional sobriety was on the line; any talk about of being "spiritual" was seriously doubtful. Three close friends who knew more about me than anyone else stepped into my emotional breach. They shared with me how they had faced and overcome similar circumstances in their lives. I spoke with at least one of them each day until the anger, fear and resentment slowly dissipated over a significant period of time.

Other organizations began to recruit me for similar positions such as Lead Counselor, Program Director or Executive Director. My confidence had been shattered as a result of being fired from my previous employment, so I accepted a counseling position with a residential treatment center. While working as the primary counselor in an addiction treatment program in Indiana, I was charged with the responsibility of counseling older adults who had been overcome by their addiction to alcohol and prescription medications. The consequences of abusing alcohol and prescription drugs among our older citizens are manifested through age, physical disabilities, depression, loneliness, a sense of isolation and uselessness, the feeling of being unwanted, unneeded and fearful. I was in my late forties at the time, and I often thought I must have looked like a teenager to them. So I would spend a great deal of time either in group or getting to know each one of these older individuals as best I could in such a short period of time (average length of stay was 30 to 45 days).

It was during this phase of my career that my mentor told me that in order to become good counselor two important skills were required: "Learn to listen and listen to learn." Looking back over my career, I realize how difficult it was for me to adhere to that sound advice. There were times when I should have been listening to the clients; instead I was mentally thinking about what I was going to say or I already had assumed they had no idea what they were talking about. I had to listen carefully to understand their concept of why they were so unhappy. It was during this process that I learned to develop my own perception of their personalities, characters and beliefs. As I listened carefully, I was better informed and could help and guide them to better understand the process of recovery. I learned to listen and, in doing so, developed the virtue of *patience*. A very dear friend once told me I had a lot of patience. I asked him how he knew and he replied, "Because you never use any."

My mentor advised me why it was important to listen and learn. "Jim," he would say, "if you listen long enough, a person will tell you what is wrong with him. And if you listen a little longer, he will tell you what he needs to do." This simple wisdom and insight has proven its weight in gold many times. If parents only had the time to do so with their children . . . oh well, that's for another time.

I was assigned as the primary counselor for a group of men and women whose average age was 60 years. We had a lot of fun interacting with each other. I watched as they rediscovered a sense of value, the joy of participation, a deep sense of belonging, and the wonders of recognition. When one of them would touch on a very personal or painful experience, the others understood the seriousness of the moment. They reached out with comforting and tender expressions of compassion, caring and love that had lain dormant for a very long time.

In this particular group was a cantankerous old gentleman. He was 82 years old at the time, still a wonderful specimen of a human being with a full head of pure white hair. He had a mind sharp as any I had ever seen, an incredibly dry sense of humor, and deep blue, sparkling eyes that captivated your attention instantaneously. The remnants of a very handsome man were still visible at 82 years of age. With a stout shillelagh always in his grasp, he could be a very intimidating-looking fellow. He was first generation Irish-American, so I was able to establish rapport with him as we discussed our family heritage. One morning in group he was particularly cantankerous in his behavior and eventually I became frustrated and confronted him head on. "John," I said, "you have been admitted to this facility because of your excessive drinking. If you're not willing to be more cooperative in group, then I'll take that to mean you're not interested in stopping drinking." John leaned forward in his chair, holding his shillelagh straight in front of him. His deep blue eyes pierced mine. "John," I continued. "If you don't stop drinking, you're going to die." There was a long silence. Finally he lowered his shillelagh, and leaning on it he said, "Son, how old is you?" I replied, "Forty-nine." "Son, I am 82 years old, and I have made it this far. By the looks of you, I seriously doubt that you'll make it." There was a howl of laughter from the other group members as I sank back into my chair. With a red face, I had to acknowledge to the group that John was right. I had forgotten an old saying I had heard long ago: "Where ignorance is bliss, it's folly to be wise."

In that brief exchange I learned more about "counseling" than in all the workshops and training I had ever participated in. John's reality at the time was that he was 82 years old, had lived a full life, so why was everyone upset with him as he came to the sunset of his life?

The group had settled down and I had remembered why I was there. After a brief pause I apologized to John and asked him if we could continue our discussion. He responded affirmatively; however, he began sharing about his family and friends rather than talking about his drinking. Soon it became evident that a very deep and sensitive man was hidden behind his cantankerous facade. His wife had passed away ten years earlier. His children now had their own families. He lived alone and was very lonely. There were many reasons he had become estranged from his children. The only contact he had with any family member was with one grandson, to whom he was very close.

As he spoke in hushed words about his grandson, tears filled his eyes, and slowly a tear rolled down his cheek. He struggled to keep his composure and seemed about to stop talking when a colleague sitting beside him reached out and gently took his hand. John paused, looked into his friend's eyes, and then the tears flowed like an uncontrollable river.

By now the rest of his colleagues had closed around him in a tight group; their own years of hidden grief were washed away by John's experience of adversity. Infirm as these folks were, their connection to each other opened the flood gates of years of loneliness, fear and isolation. It was at that moment they found the strength of character that had long been subdued by loneliness and isolation. To witness this group of people come together in a spirit of unity was almost overwhelming. They were fully alive, their collective spirit manifested by their camaraderie, empathy and compassion for each other. As composure returned to the room, each participant spoke soft and gentle words to John. Words of gratitude, encouragement and love were spoken to each other, for they had felt exactly like John.

I turned to John and said, "John, I apologize. Your right to drink or not to drink is your choice. However, when you do drink, you usually fall asleep with a cigarette in your hand, and I have been told that that has happened on a number of occasions." He nodded his head in agreement. "John," I continued, "you and your grandson love each other very much. It must be terrifying for him to think about you burning to death alone at home." I continued, "I would not be surprised if all your grandson wants for you is to have your own place, attached to his home. He wants to savor every moment he can to be in your company, but the fear of fire is terrifying to him." Again, John nodded in agreement. His eyes became teary once again; however, this time there was a softness and relief in his face. He knew what he had to do.

A few weeks later I quietly watched John and his grandson walk down the long hall as he was being discharged from the facility. His left hand was on his grandson's shoulder, and in his right hand he held the ever present shillelagh. With confidence and determination that only can be seen in a person who has discovered a purpose in life, John and his grandson stepped out into the sunlight with the knowledge that he had what he needed to enjoy the golden years of his life. The words of a song from the musical *Cats*, "A New Day Had Begun," was ringing in my ears.

I was never to know the outcome of John's experience, but I was never more certain of my own place in life. As I approach my own golden years, I have a wonderful relationship with my family and friends. Loneliness is not a part of my life today. It is the result of meeting many people like John, who in most cases unknowingly taught me the Art of Living Life.

Family

After I reenlisted in the Air Force in 1958, Irene and I got married, and shortly afterwards I headed for the Clark Field in the Philippines. Irene joined me a few months later. Our oldest daughter, Maureen, was born there. Sometime later I was reassigned to Naha Air Base, in Okinawa. Pauline, our second daughter, was born while I was stationed there, followed a year later with the arrival of our twin sons, Sean and Steven.

The conflict in South East Asia was beginning to heat up. The space program was beginning to flourish, and for this proud member of the Air Rescue Service, it was an exciting time. However, hidden from all others was the overwhelming fear of being discovered a coward. At first, alcohol was the perfect solution. A few drinks would remove the body's inner tension, and my mind would be liberated of its fears and anxieties. This sensation was so wonderful that the thought of drinking too much was never a consideration. But, over time, the wisdom of an old Chinese saying, "A man takes a drink, the drink takes a drink, the drink takes the man," was to become a reality. The hangovers began to be more frequent. The physical, mental and emotional price increased; I paid that price and had a few moments of peace. My work would be affected, and my home life would suffer severely. Despite countless resolutions to refrain from drinking, I found it impossible.

The structure of my very being had been altered. Once I took that first drink, the ability to stop of my own will was lost. It is no wonder that I eventually became that which I feared becoming, a coward. I drank to live and I lived to drink. The impact that this had on my family was beyond description. One would think that they would be destroyed physically, mentally and emotionally. This was not to be the case. Although I strongly believed they had suffered greatly from my inexcusable behavior, their character was of sufficient strength that they loved me in spite of myself. My inability to love and respect myself was overshadowed by the most destructive element of the human spirit: shame.

Yet I would not, could not, stop drinking. This hell was exacerbated by an incredible sense of guilt and shame. This, I have come to believe, is the core of my addiction. I knew I was guilty, not only of my behavior, but of my failure to change it. The incredible guilt I inflicted upon myself manifested in overwhelming feelings of loneliness, isolation and depression. When family and friends reached out to comfort and care for me, it only intensified the pain to such a point that the thought of death became an option. How could I or anyone else reach such a depth of despair that the love from loved ones in and of itself was pure torture?

I had worked in my father's pub in Scotland on Friday and Saturday nights. This was in addition to another job I'd had since I was thirteen years old. The operation of a drinking establishment in Scotland was bizarre. "Pubs," as they were called, were facilities licensed to serve alcohol during specific hours of the day: Monday through Thursday, 10:00 a.m. to 2:00 p.m. and 5:00 p.m. to 9:00 p.m.; Friday and Saturday evenings till 10:00 p.m.; closed on Sundays. The clientele was all male. Beer and lager were usually served in pint glasses (16 oz.), and alcohol was served by the dram. The bar area was standing room only, and in the men's room there was a long wall urinal.

After the local soccer matches, the patrons would rush in, and in a very short time the bar would be a mass of people shouting for a pint of beer or some other alcoholic beverage. I was surprised at how fast they consumed their drinks. I concluded that, since the pub closed at 9:00 or 10:00, depending on the day, they only had a few hours of drink. In the midst of this pandemonium, it was my job to keep the glasses washed and the beer barrels working and replaced when they ran out. Each time a bottle of alcohol was emptied, the bartender would screw the cap back on, and I would take them downstairs to the basement and invert the bottle in a cardboard box. Every so often I removed the bottles from their boxes, and, still inverted, removed the bottle cap over a open metal container and let the drips fall into it.

As the evening wore on, my job was not only to wash the beer glasses but to keep half a dozen or so almost full of beer. My dad would then grab one or two, top them off and serve them to outstretched, eager hands. As the final hour for serving approached, the frenzy to consume more alcohol was amazing. It would reach a crescendo when those words of doom rang out: "Gentlemen, last call." I would even be thrown into the fray. I would be standing at the beer taps, both of them wide open, feverishly filling pint glasses as fast as I could. "Gentlemen, please, last call." I had worked hard for four hours, but this was pure excitement the likes of which I never quite understood. I loved every second of it. "This is what it is like to be a man!"

My father's voice could be heard over the din. "Gentlemen, now gentlemen, please, the bar is closed." By now I was stationed at the exit of the establishment, having closed and locked the door on the inside as per my father's instructions. As some of the patrons moved toward the door, they would stagger out and I would lock the door again. Most of them were very happy and would say to me as they passed by me such things as "Goodnight, lad" or "You're a fine specimen of a young man — God bless you" or "Ah, you're a great son of Tommy Leonard's." For most of them, it appeared at that moment that they were happy, joyous and free. It would never occur to me that for some, misery would descend on them later in the night.

Looking back, it was 1949, and the war had been over for four years, but life in Scotland was still very difficult. Unemployment was very high. Men who had survived the horrors of the great battles were now left with nothing to do. Post Traumatic Stress Disorder had not been heard of then, but all of its ramifications were at play as surely as in those young men who survived the Iraqi/Afghanistan wars of today.

Physical, Mental and Emotional Stress

I suspect that a large number of people have untreated Physical, Mental & Emotional Stress (PMES). This is not to be confused with the Post Traumatic Stress Disorder (PTSD) diagnosis found in the DSM-IV. For many, the nightmare of 9/11 and its subsequent consequences is a prime example of post traumatic stress disorder. PTSD is not restricted to our military, law enforcement, firefighter and other first responders. Extreme trauma can occur in the most "secure" place: home, school and church.

In my thirty-five years working in the addiction field, I have become convinced that every client or patient I have worked with has suffered from some form of trauma. However, society has labeled that type of trauma as *stress*. I know that addiction can result in death or serious health injures, yet I also understand that stress can do the same. In our society attitudes toward trauma and stress are different — so different that we treat them differently. In the treatment of addiction the process begins with abstinence from all mood-altering substances, followed by various therapies, including physical exercises, good nutrition, and, in many settings, an introduction to spirituality. Unfortunately for many, returning to daily living creates an overwhelming stress, stress that is often magnified hundreds of times in the mind of the individual.

Even our political atmosphere results in subtle psychological stress, and the effect of such intense stress upon our society is very traumatic. This is exacerbated as many of our politicians and power brokers seek to destroy the character and reputation of their opponents. I call that character assassination. The schism between the "right" and "left" is not only one of religious and moral grounds, but of fear, a deep soul-wrenching fear that has become engrained in the very fiber of our soul (spirit). Has spiritual malady fallen on the most powerful nation in the world? It is not that we have turned away from God, but that we have turned away from each other. It is no wonder that a majority of the people in America do not trust each other.

We have an inherent obligation to be responsible for the well-being of others as well as of ourselves. We are certainly held accountable by each other during our participation in this life cycle. And therein may lie the root of all our troubles. For, despite our accomplishments in medicine, technology, education, wealth, and our standard of living, we are consumed by fear. Each of us has an instinct to survive, and when that instinct is threatened, we react with fear. This experience is further exacerbated by another kind of fear, a fear we create in our mind. There we can imagine all kinds of fear and in so doing practically immobilize all rational thoughts. In my own particular experience, I withdrew inwardly and desperately in an attempt to completely isolate from everyone and everything. In spite of all my efforts, I could not completely separate from everyone and everything. Even those who resort to the ultimate act of destruction, suicide, may only destroy their fear, but not their spirit.

A great fallacy for us is that we have been conditioned by a series of events to focus on the "negative." We automatically deny or close our minds to alternatives to our thinking. In my own situation, I became convinced that those who were of the Protestant faith were dangerous. The Jews were evil — after all, they crucified Christ. The English were snobs, power-hungry and persecutors of all other human beings; while we Irish were gentle folk, defenders of the faith, great educators, poets, writers and builders of the foundation of Western culture. The Germans allowed Hitler to come to power, seeking world denomination with their ally Japan. Following the defeat of Germany and Japan, it was the North Koreans, the Vietcong, Saddam Hussein, Osama Bin Laden, and the Taliban of Iran and its threat of nuclear power. Some of our most intelligent people had a knack for creating names that spoke volumes of their hatred for and prejudice against other human beings. “Kraut,” “Jap,” “Chink,” “Gook” are prime examples. Today we have such words as “redneck,” “white trash,” “queers,” “faggots” and “straight people,” and of course the “N” word. The most common words used in the English language can be the most destructive weapons we possess to attack fellow human beings.

Have we segregated ourselves into groups of people forced to coexist with each other, and are we simultaneously obligated to destroy each other by whatever means possible? Do we unwittingly destroy other people in our society and in doing so destroy ourselves? Recently, I heard a comment by a well-known reporter who covered the war in Iraq for seven years, “When you seek revenge, dig two graves, one for your enemy and one for yourself.” I understand the merits of that statement.

During my military career it was easy to develop an attitude toward my enemies. This attitude was reinforced by words that describe contempt for my enemies. Unfortunately for me, it soon permeated my daily language and behavior with friends and family. I soon discovered that I could almost destroy another’s character and sense of well-being by verbal assassination; at the same time I was aware of the insidious nature of what I was doing. This was further complicated by the strong belief that I could not stop this kind of behavior no matter how hard I tried. When I became aware that I had the choice and ability to change my behavior, wonderful things began to happen. And since realizing this phenomenon of changing my own thoughts and behavior, I have overcome this terrible contempt for my fellow man, especially those who I believed were less than me.

Often I would be so angry and resentful at someone that the thought of revenge was all-consuming. It never occurred to me that *I* was consumed physically, mentally and emotionally by such powerful feelings of hatred, manifested by intense feelings of resentment, fear and selfishness. My “miracle,” it turned out, was Irene, the mother of our children. I have now come to understand that the most powerful instinct of the human experience is motherhood. Irene first researched every piece of information she could find about alcoholism. On a number of occasions she was advised by others that there was nothing she could do. To her it was not acceptable that she could to nothing. She persisted and eventually concluded there was only one thing left to do. And that was to confront me directly. She prepared the children and, with the support of my supervisor and a counselor, set a date for the Intervention. I, of course, was completely unaware of what was to happen. On the selected day I was instructed by my supervisor to report to a particular office for an important meeting. That “meeting” was unpleasant and uncomfortable. I can unequivocally say that it was the “beginning” to the “end” of my alcoholism and simultaneously the awakening of my spirit to Recovery and Renewal. The road to Recovery, Renewal and Redemption has been long and at times arduous. But the journey to Recovery has brought me understanding and an appreciation for life, a life that was impossible for me to ever envision.

Canterbury Tails

The early morning mist covered the manicured paddocks of Canterbury Tails. The sun had not quite risen over the east paddock, but dawn was upon us. The solitude of nature reminded me of wonderful experiences from long ago. The color of the grass brought back fond memories of my childhood in Ireland. The world around me was at peace, and for a brief moment in time I was in harmony with creation, physically, mentally and emotionally. And once again I understood the essence of being "spiritual."

Visibility around the house was limited to a hundred feet in any direction. The horses and other farm animals were hidden behind a cloud of fog. The old oak trees around the house were standing guard, majestically dressed in their finery, their stout trunks covered in age-old bark, their branches wrapped in lovely green ivy, a gently gray moss hanging from their branches. Slowly this wonderful setting was to be disturbed only by the sound of silence itself, the sound that one hears when all is still, even one's thinking. Silence, those precious moments of time that can only be violated by our thoughts, will lead to the ultimate in meditation, to solitude, where life itself is at peace.

Canterbury Tails is a horse farm west of Ocala, Florida, with beautiful, manicured fields, that at first appears like a picture on a canvas. Closer observation allows me to see how each blade of grass is unique. Where each blade of grass grows, there is an abundance of life, life that interacts in ways of which few of us are ever aware. Horses quietly graze. Beautiful oak trees provide shade. Birds, squirrels and other animals complete the cycle of life each and every day.

The owners were wonderful, incredible and adorable people,

and I was fortunate to find them through a listing which mentioned their guest house was for rent. Since my focus was truly on other matters, I was at first undecided about whether to call the telephone number listed in the paper. Thinking "what the heck" I called, listened to a voice mail, left a message, hung up, and went about my day. A short time later my call was returned, and after a brief conversation, in which I told the owner about myself, my background, my present status and my purpose, he invited me to visit that afternoon. As I drove onto the farm, I was in awe; it was beyond anything I could ever imagine. But even the beautiful surroundings were to be overshadowed by the man who created the farm.

Joe was the owner of Canterbury Tails. He greeted me enthusiastically and cordially, as he would a member of his family. The awe I felt upon entering the farm was now escalating to a feeling of being *home*. I felt as though I had known this man all my life. He was to have a profound influence on my life, and over time I began to realize how significantly Joe's character and personality affected me.

Joe passed away a few years ago, and I will always remember him. He was truly a gentle man. Many a morning he would drive by and pick me up in his car and off to breakfast we would go. Our conversations were always interesting, informative and personal, like two brothers catching up after being years apart. Joe had retired from a successful career in business and was now dedicated to his wife's passion, her love of horses. Joe told me wonderful stories of being with Jackie as she participated in various horse shows across the country and overseas. Jackie was a trainer and driver of carriage horses and won a number of competitive shows during her career. She was very successful in her own business ventures, and it was a joy to see the partnership these two lovely people had created together. Like all successful couples, they had had their share of tragedy and trauma, but instead of surrendering to it, they grew through it. I will always be grateful to both of them for the privilege of sharing a part in their lives, if only for a short time. I believe with all my heart that it was here at Canterbury that the idea of writing this book began.

Evening once again is returning to Canterbury Tails. A gentle breeze blows over the green pasture, which has been fenced into meticulous paddocks. I walk among the horses as they quietly go about grazing on the lush grass. Jackie's horses are Friesians. These beautiful, majestic animals are predominately black in color and stand about 15 hands, with long tails. These are gentle but powerful creatures, magnificent in their stature, and friendly in their temperament. As I observe these lovely animals, I cannot help wondering how they came about, how each species evolved down through the centuries.

As I think of such things I become acutely aware of my surroundings. I watch birds fly, while other birds are resting on wooden fences. I hear them chirping in the distance, the lonely call of a whippoorwill. I am very aware that the sounds the birds make at evening time is far different from those at dawn. A brown tabby barn cat takes notice of me from a distance. Looking for the two small goats, I fail to see them. I suspect they are settling in for nightfall. Covering all this beauty is the majestic canopy of old oak trees, with branches covered in moss swaying with the breeze.

Serenity, that mystical moment eagerly sought by many and seldom realized, is here. This wonderful place, which is so full of activity during the day, is at the same time the center of tranquility. Horses are being trained, groomed or bathed. Still others are being attended to by a farrier or veterinarian. Stalls are being cleaned, with a fresh covering of wood chips and sawdust scattered on the floor. Fields are being mowed, equipment is being maintained, and many other routine and mundane chores are being done every day. All this is accomplished by a small group of people, who are happy and content with life. Paradoxically, serenity does not just happen; it is the result of being in harmony with ourselves, with others, and with the world around us.

It was here that the concept of spirituality blossomed into a reality of life. I had been at the mercy of fear, anxiety, worry, and depression most of my life. I had projected my internal thoughts onto my external surroundings and thus created a life of fear and depression that no human could withstand for the duration of life. When I realized that I was the creator of my thoughts and accepted total responsibility for my behavior as the direct result of acting on those thoughts, my attitude changed. I was free. The jailer of my life was a self-constructed prison, and the key to freedom was inside. When I finally took the risk and turned the key, I did not run out of my prison but moved rather cautiously, many times hesitating or stopping, as I fumbled along the path.

Canterbury Tails was my "haven." Many of us fail to see our haven because we are blinded by fear and resentment. By nature no man is alone, and sadly some of us try desperately to isolate ourselves from others; a few succeed, but many cannot exist in their isolation and exist in a life of fear, pain and loneliness. In my case, my guide was Joe. There have been many others "Guides" in life along the way, but Joe was the culmination of all that was good. His kindness, empathy and attentive ear provided the candle in my darkness, and one day I was out of the tunnel. I was completely aware of my surroundings, and for a brief moment in time I was free of self.

Shame is to Blame

The most intense emotion I have ever experienced is shame. The feeling of shame convinced me that I was totally despicable and worthless, without redemption. It was the virus of my spiritual being. Shame is a powerful form of control used by people who commit relational aggression and is also used in society as a form of overt social control. A condition or state of shame may originate externally from others, regardless of one's own experience or awareness. "*To shame*" generally means to actively shame another by behaviors designed to "uncover" or "expose" others with utterances like "Shame!" or "Shame on you!" Finally, to "*have shame*" means to maintain a sense of restraint against offending others while to "*have no shame*" is to behave without such restraint.

There are many ways one can be freed from shame. A competent psychiatrist, therapist, or counselor can guide one through an appropriate process. Consulting with a priest, minister, rabbi or cleric of one's religious faith is another way. Conversing with a close friend or someone who has confided in you their experiences with recovering from shame is also helpful. In simple terms, if one suffers from a lack of self-esteem or self-worth, it is usually an indication that shame is present. In my own recovery process, shame was seldom discussed let alone explored. I was completely ignorant of the power of shame. Only through the loving compassion of a few close friends (who were more interested in what I could become than who I believed I was), did I begin to believe that it was possible that I had some value and therefore was worthy rather than worthless. There were many times during this process when I was plagued by doubt and distrust of my own abilities. There are times when hindsight is invaluable, and I found that, during these crises of character, I only had to look back and see where I had come from to reassure myself that "this too shall pass."

"This too shall pass." I remember the first time I heard this statement. My mental reaction was, "What a stupid statement." Today, in my estimation, this phrase is the simplest statement of absolute faith, a faith that is demonstrated daily in my life. No sadness or gladness, no emotional pain or gratification, no fear or courage, no anger or serenity lasts indefinitely. Life goes on to its ultimate conclusion. So I live life and all of its experiences to the best of my ability, and my abilities strengthen with each experience.

My terrifying experiences with shame and the painful process of identifying the root causes of all my shame, followed by an intense period of healing, in the end developed one of my greatest assets: empathy.

This Native American Prayer provided the most simple and explicit understanding of shame.

Oh, Great Spirit whose voice I hear in the wind
And whose breath gives life to the world. . .
Hear Me. . .
I come to you as one of your many children.
I am small and weak.
I need your strength and your wisdom.
May I walk in beauty?
Make my eyes ever behold the red and purple sunset.
Make my hands respect the things that you have made
and my ears sharp to hear your word.
Make me wise that I may know the things that you have
taught your children . . .
The lessons you have written in every leaf and stone.

Make me strong,
not to be superior to my brother but to be able to fight my greatest enemy . . .
Myself.
Make me ever ready to come to you with straight eyes
So that when life fades as the fading sunset,
My spirit may come to you,
Without shame.

(Translated by Chief Yellow Lark, 1887)
(There are a number of variations or adaptations of this prayer.)

Shame is as old as mankind itself. The story of Adam and Eve that I heard in school was my introduction to shame. I recall asking, "Why was Eve trying to hide from God? After all, God had made her, and what was it that she did not want God to see?" I recall being told that it was her nakedness. *What is so bad about being naked?* Over time I learned that being naked was not acceptable and that God would punish me severely. Many religious groups have various rituals and dogmatic strategies that, if not complied with, often result in the offender being humiliated, castigated and excommunicated. Secrets, those thoughts and behaviors I tried to hide from God and parents, were the cancer of my soul, and no human being could relieve me of my *disgrace.* Disgrace: to be out of favor with God, an outcaste, an unworthy human being; to believe I am less than human. This belief of self was so embedded in my mind that I was beyond salvation, in both religious and humanistic terms.

Transformation

Each individual has the ability to transform himself or herself into a mentally healthy and emotionally stable human being. However, to do so will not be without pain. Physical pain occurs when our bodies are subjected to inward dysfunction and outward damage. As the body heals, it is often accompanied by intense pain, pain that may equal in intensity that which necessitates a healing process.

In simple terms, most mental and emotional pain is generated from intense feelings of fear, guilt and shame. These feelings are often manifested by such things as anxiety, poor self-image or self-esteem, and feelings of uselessness and loneliness. To identify and understand such feelings will at first seem impossible.

Understanding is the result of knowledge and experience. Learning from my own experiences and through knowledge of the experiences of others, I now possess strength of character and moral value. I am free from my self-serving attitude. I no longer overtly or covertly demand that others make me happy. It is one thing to judge others, but it is the epitome of self-righteousness to condemn them.

When I re-enlisted in the Air Force in 1958, I was assigned to Clark Field, in the Philippines, and before leaving for my new assignment, Irene McGuirr and I married. She later joined me in the Philippines where our oldest daughter, Maureen, was born. Later I was transferred to Naha Air Base, in Okinawa, Japan. During my stay there our second daughter, Pauline, was born, followed a year later by the arrival of our twin sons, Sean and Steven. The conflict in South East Asia was beginning to "heat up." The space program was beginning to flourish. As a member of the Air Rescue Service, it was an exciting time for me. It was clouded at times by an overwhelming fear of being discovered a coward. In 1963, I was reassigned to McClellan Air Force Base, in Sacramento, CA. There our youngest son, James Jude (Jimmy), was born. My reassignment to the US turned out to be a very stressful experience. Since Maureen, Pauline, Sean and Steven had been born outside the US, their nationality and citizenship came into question. I was a naturalized citizen and their mother was a British citizen. Under the law at that time, they were not eligible for US citizenship. The ruling was that I had to be a citizen for 10 years before any children (born to us outside of the United States, regardless of my military status) were eligible for US citizenship. After much frantic communication with numerous US government agencies, at the very last moment the problem was solved by the British Embassy in Manila. The children were deemed British citizens, and their mother and I, under British Law, were still subjects of the British Crown, which allowed them to be issued US visas. I felt betrayed by the United States Air Force, and for a long time I held a deep resentment toward the United States embassy, as I felt they had implied that my family was my responsibility and not the concern of the Air Force or the Department of Defense. I did not understand the mission and objectives of two distinct units of American democracy: the State Department and the Department of Defense. Since I was feeling very isolated and alone, it was "normal" for me to have a drink or two and figure this out.

Once I took that first drink, the ability to stop of my own free will was lost forever. It is no wonder that I eventually became that which I was feared the most: a coward and a drunk. I drank to live and I lived to drink. Today I know that being alone in my loneliness was the darkest period of my life. I am now acutely aware that I was "dead." What I did not know or understand was that I was spiritually dead. Many of us suffer from a similar malady. Being spiritually "dead" is manifested by deep depression, anxiety, emotional fears, loneliness, isolation, and an assortment of other behaviors. These include alcoholism, drug abuse, prescription drug abuse, overeating, anorexia and bulimia, gambling and other excessive and compulsive behaviors.

I was assigned to McClellan Air Force Base, California, and my family and I settled into a home in North Highland. Being back in the good old USA should have been a great opportunity for me to advance my career and educational development. What I did not know or refused to acknowledge was that the early stages of alcoholism had set in. Some would say I was in denial; maybe so, but I believed alcohol was not the problem. Nine years of active duty and still not a Non-Commissioned Officer. Six years earlier I had been number two on the promotion list. The day the promotion list was announced, I was passed over for someone who had only five years and had not even been in the top five for promotion. I was told not to worry, that I was number one on the next list. That list never materialized; the Air Force froze all promotions, with a few exceptions for highly skilled technicians. I was finally promoted to SSgt (E-5) around 1971 and TSgt (E-6) in 1974. Three years later I had to retire because the time limit to make MSgt (E-7) had run out for me.

This was the final blow: forced to retire, with no marketable skills for civilian life, terrified that I would be unable to take care of family — there was nothing left. A deep depression, coupled with an overpowering sense of loneliness and isolation, set in. And when my family and supervisor confronted me about my excessive drinking, I agreed with one caveat: I would do it on my own — no counseling, and no hospitalization. Six weeks later I had a complete mental and emotional psychosis and found myself confined to a hospital bed in restraints.

Humility

Knowing the best about me, without thinking I am better than you.

—Anonymous

It is now clear to me that many confuse piety with humility, believing that if they could practice piety in thought, word, and action, then humility is assured. I was to learn that what I thought was the meaning of humility was distorted by my limited knowledge of language. I knew what each word meant to me as I spoke it. I was to find out that what others heard me say was often different from what I believed I had said. Although we may speak the same language, the interpretation of our words is often influenced by culture, beliefs, regional dialect and religious teachings. And so it was with the word *humility*.

I found my truth about the word *humility*. The root word *humus* (the organic part of soil formed from decaying matter) is at the core of the word *humility*. The analogy was clear to me: the leveling of my pride, the understanding that my ego produces the organic substance of my character. The more I thought about the concept, the more difficult it was for me to comprehend it. I think the breakthrough came when I slowly began to realize how very narrow-minded and cynical I had become. I was entrenched in my past and no one was going to "convert" me to understand anything from his point of view or understand her beliefs. This entrenchment became the major block keeping me isolated and alone. The cement that bound the blocks together was fear and shame. This ensured that there was no possible escape from this self-constructed prison.

A PRAYER OF HUMILITY

Humility is perpetual quietness of heart. It is to have no trouble.
It is never to be fretted or vexed, irritable or sore;
To wonder at nothing that has been done to me.
To be at rest when no one praises me.
And when I am blamed or despised,
It is to have a blessed home in myself
where I can go to and shut the door
And kneel to my father in secret and be at peace,
As in a deep sea of calmness,
when all around and about is seeming troubled.

—Written by Andrew Murray (1828–1917),
a South African religious leader

What is humility? There are many personal definitions of humility. When I relinquished my personal definition in favor of this description I found on Wikipedia, I found that humility was *the state of being modest and respectful.*

My understanding of respect was limited to the rules and expectations that I placed on other people and institutions. Therefore, I was always in conflict with someone or something. It was only through developing an open mind, by listening to the opinion of others, and by gathering facts instead of rushing to judgment that I achieved a greater understanding of humility. Many believe that humility is a sign of weakness. Others claim that in order to be humble, one must be "saved" by a strong religious conversion. Many religious denominations — Christianity, Islam, Judaism, and others — proclaim similar dogmas. It is in the development of my character that I take complete and total responsibility for my own personal beliefs.

When I was a child I behaved like a child. Now that I am a

man, my behavior at any given moment is the truth of who I am. When I lie about my behavior, it is because I refuse to take responsibility for my behavior. When I am truly humble, I know the difference between choices and decisions. When I make a choice without any consideration for the consequences on others, then I am being selfish. When I make a decision, if it is based on the well-being of others as well as of myself, then I am selfless. We all have the ability to be humble, regardless of race, creed or sex, and I have found that the gateway to happiness is through the doors of humility.

Relationships

Life is all about relationships. While there are many definitions of the word relationship, it is the formation of two words that allowed me to grasp a simple process: relation = a connection; ship = a large vessel for carrying goods and people. From the day I was born until the day I die, I will constantly be in a relationship with someone, even if at times it may only be with myself. I have come to understand the purpose of each relationship as I experience the joy and sadness each encounter brings. My understanding of relationships is constantly changing. Unfortunately I, like many others, had believed that a "good" relationship was supposed to bring individual happiness. I had looked to others to make me happy and was often disappointed. One of the most critical flaws I had about relationships was my perception that they were easy after I got over my nervousness. To me it was just a normal function of being human. When the time came and I found myself trying to change my attitude in general, I began to explore all my ideas and concepts about how I had been living. I now firmly believe that the most important relationship any human being can experience is the recognition, acceptance and understanding of himself.

At the heart of all relationships is understanding. The human "spirit," as manifested by our spirituality, can be very elusive to understand. Spirituality is not the sole possession of a particular religious or secular group. Spirituality is the very spirit of every human being. It is the spirit that exists in all of us and is defined by each individual's own life experiences. While there is much debate about what spirit represents and as many different definitions as there are people who have experienced it, I have come to believe that all life experiences have three common attributes, which are the physical, mental and emotional dimensions of our humanness. These can be readily identified by our actions and our behaviors, but I have come to believe there is one other dimension: the spirit, better known as the human spirit — and each of us has to find our own "spirit."

In my own personal journey, many events occurred that, at the time, made little sense in my thinking; it was only in quiet reflection and meditation that I was able to discern their impact on my thinking. There is a quote from Hamlet I first read in school as a young boy. While I had no interest in Shakespeare's work at the time, the following line stuck in my mind like a recording.

"To be or not to be, that is the question."
—William Shakespeare

"To be happy or not, that is the answer."
—Jim Leonard

A fourteenth century Dalai Lama was asked, "What is the meaning of life?" "To be happy and help others," he replied. For centuries mankind has asked the same question, but there does not appear to be any universal agreement. So instead of finding the meaning of life, I chose to make life meaningful. I had held others accountable for my happiness, and I discovered many others had made the same mistake. Why and how do we do that? First consider why. We are born into a family system that is ritualistic in its behavior, and we become enmeshed in its routine. The paradox of this experience is that it is necessary for establishing a foundation for adulthood and, as that is done, sometimes unrealistic fears of how we relate to others outside our community are created. It is true that most families attempt to teach virtues to their offspring such as love, sincerity, respect, tolerance and the like. These virtues are necessary for developing strong character. Unfortunately, we are also exposed to things that hinder the development of our character. These "defects" include pride, lust, envy, retaliation, greed, laziness, and gluttony.

I am unhappy when I choose to let these "defects" in my character influence my decisions as to how I interact with others. People say such things as, "They pushed my buttons." Sadly, that statement allows the person with the buttons that got pushed to hold others accountable for their feelings. Nothing is further from the truth. Each individual's "feelings" are embedded in the belief system learned in the family of origin. As adults, our purpose in life means taking complete responsibility for our beliefs and holding ourselves accountable for our own behavior. As this is understood and accepted, the road to happiness becomes much clearer and easier to navigate. There will be "bumps" along the way. However, like commercial airline pilots, we can develop a "flight plan" or, if you like, a "life plan." First come the basic rules of flying, then lots of emphasis on safety, followed by continuous training.

What became obvious to me was that I did not know how to live. On the contrary, all I knew was how to survive, and in doing so I was living a miserable life. How do I develop a plan for living? The very essence of my life begins with learning the basic rules of life. Shortly after my birth I began to breathe on my own. Before that I was totally dependent on my mother to maintain my "life." Now I breathe independently of any other human being. My mind begins to develop with the help of the five basic senses: hearing, seeing, touch, taste and smell. I finally develop the power of reasoning and discover that my mind belongs to me, instead of the erroneous belief that I belong to my mind. So I discipline my mind over and over again by practicing the principles of compassion, tolerance and honesty. What I think is not always what I do, for by now I know and understand the consequences of my behavior.

All relationships are personal and therefore cannot be avoided. Relationships are the "heart" of our life's experiences. I have come to believe there are three fundamental relationships. My first one was with the woman who gave me life, my mother.

The second was with my father, siblings, extended family members and countless others (teachers, members of religious orders, neighbors, friendly and not so friendly people, etc.), and the third, the most difficult of the three, with self. My mother was the epitome of what psychologists for years have tried to understand, the emotional, mental and behavioral development of personality and character. In my 78 years of living, nothing has surpassed or replaced her natural ability to nurture and care for her family, to suffer and sacrifice her own desires and wants for the love of her children. Where did this incredible sense of purpose come from? I don't know. I can only suspect it comes from the most natural of all human instinct, procreation, that wonderful burden reserved for mothers.

The other two basic relationships are much different from the first. They require a much more active participation on my part. The development of my relationship with my father was significantly different from that with my mother. By observing and communicating with my father, I learned how to be a "man," and with siblings and school friends I practiced being a "man" till young adulthood. Then I was a man, or so I thought. It would be years later before I understood what it really meant to be a man. The most difficult relationship I had was the third one, the one with self. This relationship will always be influenced by the other two basic relationships. The rituals of these relationships have some things in common, namely my well-being and the well-being of others. I constantly seek to improve my understanding of life by understanding these relationships.

Accomplishing this is a very daunting task. However, a persistent and consistent effort to take a few moments each day to look at what I have accomplished and then consider the events and decisions of the day, giving attention to improvement, has been my way to improve all relationships. I conclude this daily review by recognizing a sense of gratitude for things well done; then I make a resolve to improve on those things I can do better.

Fear

Fear, of all human emotions, has the most influence on our choices and decisions. Fear dominates our daily lives and for many has so captivated them that it is impossible for them to live productive or normal lives. Mental health professionals will quickly point out that, as a population, we are constantly faced with decisions and consequences that elevate our stressful condition. For the longest period I did not know what constitutes a "normal" life. I assumed that most people knew what was normal and what was not normal. I assumed that to be normal was to live without fear. For a number of years I believed I was a coward, and the concept of living in constant fear seemed "normal." I remember the first time I heard the word "stress," and how contemptuous I felt about those who claimed to be suffering from stress. To me "stress" meant being tired or exhausted from some aspect of daily living, and all one had to do was rest and recuperate. Fear, on the other hand, was constant and so debilitating that rest was impossible.

I had endured intense fear for almost half of my life, often manifest in feelings of anxiety, panic, being overwhelmed, and, the cruelest of all, powerlessness to do anything about the fear. In many cases it was so severe that my behavior had no value for me. I just wanted some relief. Alcohol was a very convenient way to change the way I felt. Alas, over time it added insult to injury. I had reached a point where I did not have the ability to stop drinking. As an Air Force Non-Commissioned Officer coming to the end of my career, to be so humiliated by a liquid substance was the last straw. The "last straw," it turned out, was not that I would be consumed by death (although I longed for it); it was the death of my extremely stubborn nature, my defiance, resistance, and my ego-centricity.

Over the years many people have shared with me how they attempted to cope with stress, yet instead, over a period of time, they became victims of it. They then attempted to find relief through various addictions, such as the use of alcohol, prescription medications, or a combination of both. Others sought incessant sexual activity, illicit drugs, obsessive control, hoarding, possessiveness, and countless other forms of behavior, all with the same focus: to overcome fear.

President Roosevelt said it succinctly, ". . . the only thing we have to fear is fear itself." Those words, uttered so many years ago when the nation struggled in the darkness of the Great Depression, are just as applicable today as they were then. There is one huge difference, however. In President Roosevelt's time, the country's focus was on what was in front of it, the common and clearly identifiable enemy of economic hardship, and the people united in common cause to restore prosperity for all. Today, as a nation we are so divided that many of our citizens do not trust their neighbors, their local business dealers, or — most confusing of all — the federal government. Most will vote to re-elect their representatives but completely distrust all others elected by their fellow citizens. Our faith in our government is practically nonexistent because we believe our neighbors are gullible and irresponsible citizens. As a result, many fear the encroachment by others on our "liberties." They threaten our religious freedoms by insisting we accept their beliefs. Our social order, our security, our democracy have been devalued, and we have become a second-class power. Is Pogo right? "We have met the enemy, and he is us"?

"The only thing we have to fear . . ." — and people play on that fear as they struggle to maintain power and exert their will, regardless of party affiliation. First and foremost, I had to understand fear on a personal level. I had to recognize that the source of all my fears came from within. I assure you this was no easy task. Fear itself dogged my every step as I sought to break loose from its chains, and I did break loose. To break free from fear took time and hard work. I soon realized I was not alone in this struggle, and, by shoving false pride aside, I allowed others to share with me how, through persistence and practice, they had broken loose from the chains of fear that had bound them for so long.

Spirituality and Altruism

For sixty years some of the most profound influences on my life had been World War II, the Vietnam War (in which I had a small part), the Iraq and Afghanistan wars (in which my granddaughter, Brenda, earned the Bronze Star with "V" for Valor). Untold millions, military and civilian men and women, died during that period, and millions of others suffered horrendous physical, mental and emotional trauma. War is truly the ultimate evil, and it is waged by men upon men. It is not natural for people to kill their young. Sadly, it is people in power who send other people's sons and daughters to do battle, while proclaiming God and Country.

There were other, more positive, experiences in my life; unfortunately, it was many years later before I fully understood and appreciated them. Among those experiences were the births of my five children; their many accomplishments as they struggled with the joys and tragedies in their own lives; the privilege of playing a very small supporting role in Projects Mercury, Apollo and Gemini, which culminated in man landing on the moon; the Hubble Telescope, which opened up the universe beyond my imagination; the evolution of the Internet, allowing instant communication around the world; and countless other remarkable achievements that man has made during my lifetime.

Throughout these years, one serious question still haunted me: Is there a God? At times, events would occur and others would say, "See? That's God working anonymously." But inside I would cry out, *If God is "good and kind," then why is God working anonymously?* In the country of my birth, most of its troubled history (at least 400 years) has centered on two profound issues: Irish independence and religious choice. Ireland had been subjected to British rule for centuries, and Ireland's population was predominately Roman Catholic; the religious leader was the pope. In Britain, the population predominately belonged to the Church of England or Protestant denominations; the religious leader was the ruling king or queen. So bitter was the conflict that people died for their beliefs and many others ended up living in squalor. It appears as if history is repeating itself throughout the world. In Christian, Jewish, and Muslim communities, cross-rivalries seek to dominate each other. Believers and non-believers, Shiite and Sunni, Jew and Palestinian still struggle for land and identity. Taking a closer look at each specific group, one will find tremendous struggles within each one to assert power. Most sectarian and non-sectarian leaders still have not acquired the skills to manage the awesome responsibility of governmental power. Still, in the midst of these leaders are people who strive to offer some balance to mankind.

Mark Twain wrote a short story called "The War Prayer." It was recommended to me a long time ago. When I finally read the story, it helped me to open my mind to a better understanding of "God." I believe my unhappiness in the past consisted of an internal and intellectual struggle about God. "Is there or is there not a God?" While many of my friends tried to help, it was hopeless. Finally I realized that I had to look at why I was so unhappy. I came to realize that it was my insistence, actually my demand, that "God" and others accountable make my life happy, regardless of my behavior. This realization opened the possibility that there was hope for me in finding happiness.

What is hope? A word used throughout our daily lives, but I suspect without much thought. "I hope you get well" or "I hope you succeed" or "I hope you find happiness." *Hope* used in this way alludes to an expectation that something good will happen. "I hope he dies" or "I hope he gets what's coming to him": *hope* used in this context indicates a deep resentment. I had no idea that the language I used (and also how I created thought patterns) could have such an impact on my attitude and behavior in life. How does anyone understand the implications of the use and perceptions of words, when no one fully explains it? Most people assume that others understand precisely what is said to them, and, if not, the result is that we can be judged as "stupid."

While I was on active duty, my greatest fear was that I would be a coward, that in great moments of fear or conflict I would become immobilized and not protect myself or my comrades. My thinking was: to be a coward is to be regarded as a non-entity, a nothing, or something other than human. I came to that conclusion in my childhood after hearing stories of heroes and traitors in my native country, about the troubles, and the condemnation of other Irishmen who turned against their families and friends by spying or informing on them. The movie *The Informer*, with Victor McLaglen in the lead role, is forever locked in my memory. He plays the role of an Irishman who informs on his best friend for 20 pounds ($80.00) so he and his girlfriend can go to America. I must have been seven or eight years old at the time I first saw the movie. For me it was the ultimate great sadness and the epitome of cowardly behavior. Would I end up like him? I would say these words to myself, "Please, God, don't let me become a coward." Added to these thoughts was my inner struggle about the existence of God.

I suppose there are many ways in which humans cope with the stress of fear, anxiety, loneliness and hopelessness. For me it was spirits, liquid spirits. From my late 20s till my early 40s, alcohol was to be my only recourse for escape. Sometimes I made clear and succinct choices to drink. On other occasions I had no conscious idea why I took that first drink, yet I know today I did make that choice. Often I would recall the simple request of my dad: "Be careful of the drink." By the time I reached the point of trying to be careful about my drinking, it was too late. It was at this point that I was true to the Chinese proverb, "The man takes a drink, the drink takes a drink, and the drink takes the man." In other words, I drank because I wanted to, then I drank because I needed to, and finally I drank because I had to.

While my behavior was irresponsible, destructive and extremely self-centered, a great metamorphosis (unknown to me) was at work, one that created great suffering for many people around me. It is by no coincidence that what I was drinking is generally is regarded as "spirits." What I realize now was that the addiction to alcohol (and how it manifested itself in my life) was a part of my journey to seek spirituality. I have come to realize that most people associate spirituality with a God of their understanding, and others associate it with some central purpose in their life.

To be human is to be part of a highly intelligent species that inhabits this planet. There is evidence that when Homo sapiens first appeared on earth (either through creationism or evolution), humans that came after, generation after generation, broadened their ability to understand. At the dawn of the 21st century, our ability to discern and understand the workings of the mind is at the threshold of human discovery. Down through the ages, spirituality was the sole domain of men who sought the meaning of life. For others it was the vehicle that they used to impose their will on others. Women, for most of humankind's existence, have been subservient to men, and in some societies that is still the norm. Fortunately, human beings, men and women, have always been driven by curiosity and a longing for our communities. The result has been a change of attitude in the male-dominated religious institutions. Women have become part of the clergy and, in some denominations, the spiritual leaders of their congregations.

In his letter to Bill W., Dr. C. G. Jung advanced the formula "spiritus contra spiritum," that is, the alcoholic's "craving for alcohol [is] the equivalent, on a low level, of the spiritual thirst of our being for wholeness, expressed in medieval language: the union with God." Alcoholism, often treated as medical disease, is much more than that. It is a spiritual illness that consumes all aspects of the alcoholic's life. Alcohol becomes the *breath* (spiritus) of life to the alcoholic. He becomes a tormented human being, and each drink takes him further down the path to self-destruction. Ironically, the very substance that he now craves to relieve him of his self destruction is killing him, physically, mentally, emotional and spiritually.

The word *spiritual* has many meanings. It is rooted in the Latin word *spiritus,* meaning "breath." The context in which this word is used falls into two categories: metaphysical or metaphorical. Metaphysics is a branch of philosophy concerned with the fundamental nature of being. Religious organizations have very specific, and in some cases unwavering, dogmatic requirements for the individual to be accepted into their fellowship. "God" is at the heart of religious organizations, and many hold other religious groups as heretics, fools or evil.

Metaphors are figures of speech in which a term or phrase is applied to something that is not literally applicable in order to suggest a resemblance. An example would be the following: *The path to resentment is easier to travel than the road to forgiveness.*

Today many people are tormented by life's demands, and in many cases "God" has failed to deliver them from adversity. Secularism for many is their distinct choice. Yet this still does not solve the problem; it only exacerbates it. While proponents of these two extremes debate and argue the virtues of their beliefs, far too often distrust, dislike, prejudice, resentment and fear make it almost impossible to bridge the vast chasm that exists between such groups.

Man's Search for Meaning, by Dr. Viktor Frankl, is the

seminal book of man's inhumanity to his fellow man. Dr. Frankl was a survivor of the Holocaust and lived to become a world-renowned psychiatrist. He writes passionately and with great sensitivity about his experiences living in such horror few of us will ever comprehend. According to Dr Frankl, three destructive elements come together to dehumanize a person: the shock that a person feels as he finds himself thrust into an environment that is unreal, followed by fear so intense and overwhelming that the individual appears to lose all sense of human emotion, and, finally, apathy. Apathy: the complete absence of all human emotion.

Dr. Frankl believed that life never ceases to have meaning. Even in the midst of such horror, if one cannot find meaning for living, then one is doomed. He concluded that every moment in life has meaning and that, while still living, we have choices.

> We stumbled on in the darkness, over big stones and through large puddles, along the one road leading from the camp. The accompanying guards kept shouting at us and driving us with the butts of their rifles. Anyone with very sore feet supported himself on his neighbor's arm. Hardly a word was spoken; the icy wind did not encourage talk. Hiding his mouth behind his upturned collar, the man marching next to me whispered suddenly: "If our wives could see us now! I do hope they are better off in their camps and don't know what is happening to us."
>
> That brought thoughts of my own wife to mind. And as we stumbled on for miles, slipping on icy spots, supporting each other time and again, dragging one another up and onward, nothing was said, but we both knew: each of us was thinking of his wife. Occasionally I looked at the sky, where the stars were fading and the pink light of the morning was beginning to spread behind a dark bank of clouds. But my mind clung to my wife's image, imagining it with an uncanny acuteness. I heard her

> answering me, saw her smile, her frank and encouraging look. Real or not, her look was then more luminous than the sun which was beginning to rise. (Dr. Viktor E. Frankl, *Man's Search for Meaning*)

Viktor Frankl and Tilly Grosser were married in December 1941. Nine months later, in September 1942, he, his wife and his parents were deported to Theresienstadt Concentration Camp. Only Dr. Frankl survived, having spent time also in the Auschwitz, Kaufering and Türkheim concentration camps (both affiliated with Dachau Concentration Camp). Where did Frankl find the strength, let alone the courage, to survive such horrible and terrifying living conditions? It is almost impossible for me to comprehend such strength and courage. When I first read Dr. Frankl's book (I had then been sober about five years), it touched me so deeply that it rekindled and renewed my spirit and gave me inspiration, with the hope that life and happiness were possible, if I worked at them.

I recall seeing the movie *To Hell and Back*, the story of Audie Murphy, the most decorated soldier of WWII. Oh, if I could only do half of what he did, even just one of his heroic accomplishments, then I would feel vindicated; however, that was not meant to be. There were many others who displayed courage beyond my understanding, men like John McCain, Martin Luther King, Jr., Gandhi, and Nelson Mandela; and women like Florence Nightingale, Susan B. Anthony, Mother Teresa, and Rosa Parks.

I now know that spirituality requires courage, and the irony is that fear is the doorway to courage. So how do I, so terrified with fear, open the door to courage? Nothing made sense to me for the longest time. One of the disciplines I have embraced is to review my life on an annual basis. One small event continually showed up in my review. I always assumed it was just one of those nice little things people do for each other. I was still searching for the "big event" that would make a significant impression on my thinking and change my life forever.

During 1977, in the midst of my mental health problems and alcohol addiction, fear was my constant companion. After I had been discharged from hospital, two men (whom I had never met) came to see me on a regular basis. They said all they were interested in was to see if I could go through the day without a drink. I am sure there were times when I said yes and other times I probably said I did not think so. On those days they always returned later to say hello. As for other topics of conversation, I have no recollection of any, but I stayed sober during a period of nine months. What was the significance of their daily visits? They expected absolutely nothing in return for visiting with me; they were only interested that I stayed sober that day. My mind could not comprehend such behavior; I was somewhat emotionally conflicted but soon found myself looking forward to their visits. My intense fear became less and less acute, and it seemed to disappear during their visits. I have come to believe that every human being has a basic spiritual need, and for me it was (and still is) a sense of belonging, participation with others, and recognition from others. These two men, by their simple act of humanity (love) for me, became the epitome of spirituality. It was that simple.

> **Altruism**: "The concern for the welfare of others. It is a virtue in many cultures and the core aspect of various religious traditions. However, the concept of 'others' as the object of concern can vary within cultures and religions." (*Wikipedia*, www.wikipedia.org)

I believe that altruism is the opposite of selfishness. It is the absence of any compensation or benefit, direct or indirect. Those two men, who came to see me each day after I was released from the psychiatric ward, were the best examples of altruism I had ever experienced. I have tried to emulate their example in my daily life, but at the end of the day I feel as though I fall short, only to try again the next day.

According to Wikipedia, most if not all of the world's religions promote altruism as a very important moral value. The following represents a summary of some religions' concepts of altruism.

Christianity

Altruism is central to the teachings of Jesus Christ as told in the Sermon on the Mount. From biblical to medieval Christian traditions, tensions between self-affirmation and other-regard were sometimes discussed. In his book, *Indoctrination and Self-deception*, Roderick Hinder tries to shed light on these tensions by contrasting them with impostors of authentic self-affirmation and altruism, by analysis of other-regard within creative individuation of the self, and by contrasting love for the few with love for the many. Love confirms others in their freedom, shuns propaganda and masks, assures others of its presence, and is ultimately confirmed not by mere declarations from others but by each person's experience and practice from within.

Though it might seem obvious that altruism is central to the teachings of Jesus, one important and influential strand of Christianity would qualify this. St. Thomas Aquinas states that we should love ourselves more than our neighbor. His interpretation of the Pauline phrase is that we should seek the common good more than the private good, but this is because the common good is a more desirable good for the individual. "You should love your neighbor as yourself" is interpreted by St. Thomas as meaning that love for ourselves is the exemplar of love for others. He does think, though, that we should love God more than ourselves and our neighbor, taken as an entirety, more than our bodily life, since the ultimate purpose of love for our neighbor is to share in eternal beatitude, a more desirable thing than bodily well-being.

Judaism

Judaism defines altruism as the desired goal of creation. Rabbi Abraham Isaac Kook stated that love is the most important attribute in humanity. This is defined as bestowal, or giving, which is the intention of altruism. This can be altruism towards humanity that leads to altruism towards the creator. Kabala defines God as the force of giving in existence. Rabbi Moshe Chaim Luzzatto in particular focused on the "purpose of creation" and how the will of God is to bring creation into perfection and adhesion with this upper force.

Modern Kabala focuses on how society could achieve an altruistic social framework. It proposes that such a framework is the purpose of creation, and everything that happens is to raise humanity to the level of altruism, the love for one another.

Buddhism

Altruism figures prominently in Buddhism. Love and compassion are components of all forms of Buddhism, and both are focused on all beings equally: the wish that all beings be happy (love) and the wish that all beings be free from suffering (compassion). "Many illnesses can be cured by the one medicine of love and compassion. These qualities are the ultimate source of human happiness, and the need for them lies at the very core of our being." (Dalai Lama)

Since "all beings" include the individual, love and compassion in Buddhism are outside the opposition between self and other. It is even said that the very distinction between self and other is part of the root cause of our suffering. In practical terms, however, because of the spontaneous self-centeredness of most of us, Buddhism encourages us to focus love and compassion on others, and thus can be characterized as "altruistic." Many would agree with the Dalai Lama that Buddhism as a religion is kindness toward others.

Jainism

The fundamental principles of Jainism revolve around the concept of altruism, not only for humans but for all sentient beings. This religion preaches the view of *ahimsa* — to live and let live — thereby not harming sentient beings, i.e., uncompromising reverence for all life. Jainism considers all living things to be equal. Jainism introduced the concept of altruism for all living beings, from extending knowledge and experience to others to donation, giving oneself up for others, non-violence and compassion for all living things.

Jainism prescribes a path of non-violence to progress the soul to this ultimate goal. Jains believe that, to attain enlightenment and ultimately liberation, one must practice ethical principles (major vows) in thought, speech and action. With consistent practice, it will be possible to overcome the limitations gradually, accelerating the spiritual progress.

Islam and Sufism

In Sufism, the concept of altruism is the notion of "preferring others to oneself." For Sufis, this means devotion to others through complete forgetfulness of one's own concerns. The importance lies in sacrifice for the sake of the greater good. Islam considers those practicing altruism as abiding by the highest degree of nobility. A constant concern for Allah results in a careful attitude towards people, animals, and other things in this world. This concept was emphasized by Sufi mystics, who paid attention to the difference in dedication to Allah and dedication to people. Sufi philosophy states, "We love the creature, because of The Creator." In practice, altruism is an Islamic ideal.

Sikhism

Altruism is essential to the Sikh religion. When a fellow Sikh attended the troops of the enemy, he gave water to both friends and foes who lay wounded on the battlefield. Some of the enemy began to fight again, and some Sikh warriors were annoyed because he was helping their enemy. Sikh soldiers brought the Sikh to their Guru and complained of his action that they considered counterproductive to their struggle on the battlefield. "What were you doing, and why?" the Guru asked. "I was giving water to the wounded because I saw your face in all of them," the Sikh replied. The Guru responded, "Then you should also give them ointment to heal their wounds. You were practicing what you were coached in the house of the Guru."

Altruism as an ideal may never be fully achieved, but it should be strived for. The average person, in the midst of living life, may see altruism as contrary to personal and family survival. However, understanding the basic premise of altruism will greatly enhance one's search for personal and spiritual growth, which becomes the cornerstone of happiness. Throughout my life, I rarely heard the word *altruism*, let alone understood it. Charity, on the other hand, was more practical and easier to practice. Altruism was left to various sects within religious bodies, such as monks, brothers and nuns.

Religious groups are made up of people who have specific fundamental beliefs and practices generally agreed upon by the members of that group. Spirituality, on the other hand, may be at the very core of our human existence, and therefore only the individual can fully comprehend, understand and be responsible for his or her personal beliefs around spiritually. In my experience, my church dictated its concept of spirituality (God), and to rebel against this was considered heresy. In extreme cases it was seen as defiance against God and Church, and the heretic was excommunicated or, in some cases, condemned to death.

Personality, Character and Communication

Each of us has developed, throughout our lifetime, our *character and personality.* Character is the spirit of each person; personality is the outward demonstration of that spirit. Each person's character is determined by moral qualities, ethical standards, and a set of principles. Our personalities are the combination of inner and outer characteristics that determine the impression we make upon others. The content of my character and the development of my personality are intrinsically entwined.

The personality and character of each person is extremely important in the business world. Most businesses know a great deal about their customers' likes and dislikes. *The New York Times* wrote an article (Nov 2004) that suggests that Wal-Mart knows just about every detail about potential customers' habits. Others suggest that the U.S. Government knows more about its people than people know about themselves. People are often confronted with choices and decisions that create stress in their daily lives. My experience has shown (and I've seen this in other people) that stress has now reached abnormal levels, and it contributes negatively to the physical, mental and emotional well-being of ourselves, our families, our communities and, I fear, our nation as a whole. So it is not surprising that the average person has very little understanding of how to be happy.

I was sober for about five years and still very unhappy and miserable. I had tried everything to change or alter my attitude, but to no avail. Slowly I became aware that what I was doing was not working and probably never would. Now hopeless in spirit, I had two choices: suicide or turn to an old friend. A few years earlier I had met a retired Army Master Sergeant in the fellowship of AA. I remember thinking, I'll talk to Joe, and if he can't give me the answer, then I know what I must do. Joe had the answer, and to achieve it I had to take complete responsibility for what I thought, what I did, and what I believed. In order to accomplish this, I had to relearn basic moral principles and enhance my understanding of the virtues that are at the core of all my beliefs. This raised very serious problems not only for me but also for many individuals — and society at large. What are these principles? Where do I find them? How shall I learn them? And the biggest issue of all, who can I trust to tell me and show me the meaning of these principles? Many will argue that the Bible, the Koran and the Torah are the primary sources for virtues. For over five thousand years most religious scholars, philosophers and spiritual advisers have been speaking of such common terms as humility, altruism, love and charity. It was with child-like faith (not needing proof) that I believed these virtues are in all of us and therefore in me. The flame of hope just glowed a little brighter.

When I open my mouth to say something, I know what the words mean to me. I don't know what the listeners will hear. Their perceptions of what was said will be determined by their own belief systems. To complicate matters, most people think faster than they speak and therefore are busily constructing a response based on what they think they hear. Living life is dependent on learning skills of communication. In our society, the most common form of communication is speech. We first learn to shape our words from our parents. Later as we enter school, our form of speech is greatly influenced by our peers. This is further complicated by the tone and emphasis we place on words as we have heard expressed by our parents in and around our home. In our society, dialect, culture and religious beliefs play a major influence in our comprehension of language. I began in my search for happiness by simply using a dictionary. I was initially surprised to find out how my past experiences had greatly influenced my understanding of words.

In the beginning I was quite embarrassed to ask for clarification of some words used in daily communication. I remember my first trip through the state of Alabama. Two military comrades and I had left Sacramento, California, bound for Maxwell Air Force Base near Montgomery, Alabama, for training. Although it was a long drive, I was very excited about crossing the United States by car. We had stopped in a small rural town somewhere in Alabama to fill up the car with gas, and I decided to go into the little gas station to get a Coke.

Sitting behind a small wooden counter was a white-haired lady, who said something I did not quite understand. In front of the counter was a metal container filled with ice and various assortments of soft drinks. I retrieved a bottle of Coke, placed it on the counter top, paid for it, turned around and started to exit the store. I was almost at the door when I a voice called out, "Y'all come back." I turned around and walked back to the counter and said to the lady, "Yes, Ma'am." She looked at me in what I thought was a somewhat strange manner and then said, "Young man, you're not from around these parts, are you?" "No," I replied. "And you're not from up North, are you?" "No," I said. There was a twinkle in her eye as she asked, "Where are you from?" "Ireland," I replied. Her face broke out in a broad smile. "I thought so. Here we say 'y'all come back' when we are parting company. I hope you enjoy your visit to our lovely state and southern hospitality." A little embarrassed, I thanked her for her kindness. I have never forgotten that experience. I have discovered, as the years have gone by, that we all have a language rooted in culture and family beliefs. That language, if not understood on a personal level, is often misstated and often misunderstood. The simplest way to improve one's ability is

"Listen to Learn and Learn to Listen." In a world constantly obsessed by speed and technology, this basic rule of communication is often lost in the noise of our modern world. I am a product of the analog world, now living in the digital world. The transition from one to the other may have affected the most common form of communications, speech. During the last thirty years in my work with many people, I became acutely aware that, although we "speak" the same language, often we interpret words differently, thus causing much confusion. It seems to me that, as each person speaks, the speaker assumes that the listeners understand precisely the meaning of each word. In this digital age time is so valuable that there is no time for clarification of what has been said. Most people go about their day convinced they heard what was said.

Happiness

"To be or not to be, that is the question."

—William Shakespeare

The answer, it turns out, is simple: "To be happy or not to be happy." The reality is that the responsibility for my happiness rests entirely within me. It took almost a lifetime to accept that reality. For most of my life I always held others accountable for my happiness. In order to understand happiness, I had to first understand what made me unhappy. In reviewing my life experiences, it became abundantly clear that I had more unhappy events than happy ones. I suspect most of us are more familiar with the feelings of unhappiness than of happiness. So I began to look at the reasons why I was unhappy.

With pen in hand, I listed a number of words that could best describe my feelings of being unhappy. At first it appeared to be a useless task. However, over a period of time I was able create a clear picture of what made me unhappy, and it came down to one basic reason: people. The primary cause of all my unhappiness was my inability to form a lasting relationship with another human, which included a relationship with self. My sense of being different, therefore unhappy, began in my school years. I recall during my third grade class participating in a spelling bee and failing to spell the word *two* correctly. I spelled it "to."

I remember my class mates laughing as I sat down. The intense feelings I experienced (as I later understood) were humiliation and rejection. I began to perceive that other people's behavior, in their verbal expressions and their body language, was in direct response to the way I spoke and behaved. At first it was my accent (a mixture of Irish and Scottish dialects), in addition to my lack of education, poor communication skills, and clumsy social skills. As time went by, these conditions got worse until I was convinced that there was something seriously wrong with me. I would often reflect about negative incidents in the past that seemed to confirm how stupid I had become. In the final analysis, I came to believe that, if I could get people's approval, then and only then would I feel that sense of belonging in the human race. Unfortunately, it had to be every person I had met, and that was impossible to achieve.

Being in the Air Force was a great opportunity for me to relocate to different parts of the world, and most of my military career was spent overseas. My life was confined to a closed military community. Not only did I belong there, but I was allowed to participate and be recognized. Money was always in short supply, and I had convinced myself that I would never make much money. However, I needed money to impress my friends. So I used most of what I had to mingle with them. In the end, the impression I made on my friends was more important than taking care of my family.

The failure to advance significantly in my military career was a devastating blow to my sense of self. I also felt that it was impossible for me to complete my education. I was convinced that I was somehow mentally incompetent. Looking back, I realized that my attitude was determined by my core beliefs, and these negative beliefs were further strengthened by religious indoctrination in my childhood. Born into a loving Catholic family, it never occurred to me to question any instruction given to me by early educators about the laws of God. My understanding at the time was that these laws were irrevocable, and the wrath of God was eternal damnation to those who broke the commandments. I had broken all of them before I was fifteen yet never had experienced sex until I was twenty-five years old. What the hell! How was I ever to get free of this life of condemnation?

Fortunately, many men and women came into my life over

the years who told me there was a solution to my transgressions. Some suggested that I turn my life over to Jesus Christ, for he had died for my sins. Others suggested a number of other religious or "spiritual" practices. Unfortunately, they all required beliefs created by other teachers. (Remember, my brain by now was conditioned to believe that I was not teachable, that I was a moron.)

My daily life had become routine to the point of boredom; it had no value. I now realize that there were many moments that could have had a significant effect on my perception of life. But my vision was blinded by a distorted image of self. Self-awareness is a doubled-edged sword: either I am aware of my goodness or I am aware of my evil characteristics. "Live" spelled backwards is "evil," and I was sure living a life backwards. To live backwards is the epitome of unhappiness. The definition of backwards is to live in the past.

The constant living in my past, the what-ifs in my life, the shame of events long ago, and the subtle prospect that life (as I perceived it) would never change — all these led me into deep despair. Alcohol had become the only recourse that had helped me endure this miserable life, until it also became a part of my constantly miserable existence. Then several events occurred that were to become the catalyst for the ongoing changes in my life: I experienced a mental breakdown, a period of mental rehabilitation, and the realization that I could not drink like other people. Then came the daily visits from the two men whose only interest was me going through the day abstaining from alcohol. They demanded nothing of me, just the privilege of stopping by my office for a few minutes each day and saying, "Can you go the rest of the day without a drink?" Some days I would say yes; other days I was not so sure. On those days they would return later and check on me. Nine months later I returned to the United States, and very soon realized I was still emotionally distraught.

While in Germany, I had attended a few AA meetings. What was remarkable about that experience was there were no rules or expectations, and, although nervous at first, I found a temporary sense of relief. I returned to the US with my family and settled near Abilene, Texas. We knew no one. I was suffering severe anxiety, and at times I was immobilized by fear. We had no money, and I was terrified I would have another mental breakdown and drink again. In desperation, I walked a number of miles to an AA meeting, not knowing what they could do for me, yet desperate for anything.

Nothing remarkable happened that day, yet the paradox was that I did not drink or have a breakdown. So I became a regular attendee at AA meetings. After some time, I made a couple of very close friends and became willing to rely on them to support me through my daily emotional upheavals. For the next five years I remained sober and slowly began to believe in the phenomenon called "hope." However, my emotional swings caused tremendous stress on my family. The guilt and shame became so intense that I felt constant thoughts of suicide.

One night, sitting in a car with the mother of my children outside an AA meeting hall, I knew I had to leave, to escape, to get away. I was convinced that I was going to have a complete mental breakdown and terrified of what I might do. All I remember to this day was getting on a bus going to Beaumont, Texas. I was still able to stay sober for a few more years and maintain some semblance of emotional stability. However, I was becoming more aware that any possibility of finding happiness was my responsibility. The problem was how to find happiness. During this period of my life I remained a regular attendee at AA meetings, but my attitude still remained full of doubt and self-pity.

The twelve steps of my recovery program taught me to take responsibility for my own sobriety. I learned the significance of three essential "principles": Honesty, Open-Mindedness and Willingness. For twenty-three years I had followed directions issued by others. Now there were no directions given; it became my responsibility to practice these three principles in my daily life. The irony was, no one could drink and get drunk for me anymore than anyone could stay sober for me. During early sobriety my life was still chaotic. In the midst of chaos, I remained abstinent. The present chaos was, at best, more tolerable than the chaos I had been living in my past.

As time wore on, I became aware that I was becoming more settled, less stressed, and, to my surprise, I comprehended serenity. At first it was of short duration, but then it was obvious to me that, the more I practiced these "principles," the longer the periods of serenity I experienced. It was during this phase that I discovered a simple secret: all I had to do was to review my life each day, seeing where I had accomplished some worthwhile things and becoming aware of things I could have done better. I soon realized, if I did this simple exercise each night, I could rest better. Eventually I became convinced that the purpose of rest was to renew three significant areas in my life: my physical, mental and emotional well-being. In doing so, I woke up most mornings feeling fully rejuvenated, with a grateful attitude to embrace the day.

These simple exercises brought untold rewards and the most surprising thing of all: Happiness. Happiness had never entered my mind. Peace of mind, serenity and spirituality was what I sought. Finding spirituality became an obsession and part of that obsession was an internal motivation to please the God of my childhood. That thought was still lurking in the dark shadows of my mind. As I "sought" this spirituality, I came across words that I was convinced I understood. However, since doubt has always been part of my character, I decided to use a dictionary, and to my surprise I discovered I often had distorted the true meaning of words. This turned out to be of incredible relief to me, for I found out I was not *stupid.* All I needed was a standard dictionary, and the dictionary clarified for me the word "ignorant." I was bereft of knowledge about how to live. In contrast, I always believed that to be stupid was to be nothing.

I now believe that, although most of us speak a common language, we all have our own historical and cultural translations. I slowly began to understand I was neither stupid nor a moron. I began to use a dictionary, and things began to make sense. One of the words I heard as part of the "recovery" language was *humility*. At first I thought it meant piety, and once again the memory of my childhood religious upbringing reared its ugly head. I was never pious; that was the luxury of Popes and Saints, and I was condemned a long time ago. In the dictionary I discovered that the word *humility* had more than one meaning. I was free to take responsibility for what I wanted to believe. I was no longer enslaved to what I had been conditioned to believe.

To be humble is to be of the earth, no greater or smaller than any other human being. Each of us has the ability to achieve great things, but our characters are flawed. Being humble is to know the best about me without thinking I am the best. With this understanding, the scabs of resentment, fear, and dishonesty began to fall away and to be replaced with serenity, courage and wisdom.

In the musical *Cats* I still hear the beautiful voice of Ms. Elaine Paige as she sings:

Burnt out ends of smoky days, the stale cold smell of morning.
The street lamp dies, another night is over, and another day is dawning.
Touch me.
It's so easy to leave me all alone with the memory
of my days in the sun.
If you touch me you'll understand what happiness is.
Look, a new day has begun.

—*Cats*, composed by Andrew Lloyd Weber

We will have joys and tribulations in this life, but the one thing I found that we need above all others is each other. In needing others, I became *part* of the human experience. I was no longer *apart* from my fellow man. ***I now know what happiness is.***

About the Author

Jim Leonard was born in Ireland and immigrated to the US in 1952. He enlisted in the US Air Force where he spent most of his 23 years of active duty, as a survival specialist.

He credits that experience to bringing to the surface his innate ability to establish a rapport with people in pain and suffering. Jim found his own recovery towards the end of 1976 and was supported by a group of people who taught him the responsibility of living a happy and useful life. He retired from active duty in 1977 and entered the field of addiction services.

Since then he has accumulated over 35 years' experience and he has held numerous positions of responsibility and leadership including: Executive Director, Program Developer, Family Program Director, Spiritual Advisor, and Residential Adolescent and Adult Counselor.

Jim now devotes his life to providing intervention and consulting services to families in need. He is the founder and director of The Art of Living Life, Inc. a non-profit organization that is committed to assisting those in need of physical, mental and emotional well-being.

He has developed a holistic approach to areas of responsibility, spirituality, and relationship issues which, he believes are the underlying issues present in addiction and other traumas.

Jim conducts seminars, workshops, lectures, retreats and individual consulting. His passion has been and continues to be to assist in personal healing, allowing the individual to achieve a healthy attitude toward life in their endeavor to live out their true potential.

CPSIA information can be obtained at www.ICGtesting.com
Printed in the USA
BVOW11s1558091213

338502BV00004B/10/P

9 780988 417014